MY
BROTHER
DEATH

Books by Cyrus Sulzberger

MY BROTHER DEATH

WHAT'S WRONG WITH U.S. FOREIGN POLICY

THE BIG THAW

SIT DOWN WITH JOHN L. LEWIS

MY
BROTHER
DEATH

by Cyrus Sulzberger

Harper & Brothers, Publishers, New York

CONTENTS

"As those old Romans robbed all the cities of the world, to set out their bad-sited Rome, we skim off the cream of other men's wits, pick the choice flowers of their tilled gardens . . . lard lean books with the fat of others' works . . . pilfer out of old writers to stuff up new Comments . . . as I have done."

ROBERT BURTON, *Anatomy of Melancholy*

ONE

The Splendor of Death
on the Mountain

THE GREEK ISLAND of Spetsais, which I like to
think of as my island, is a small, wooded rock that
rises gently out of the Argolic Gulf. Although it lies
just off the Spartan shore, the symmetry of Spetsais
is an Attic symmetry: harmonious and pure; land,
sea and sky. When the sun shines upon its white
houses, its white churches and the white sails of its
fishing boats, the island gleams with life's intimate
details.

Toward summer's end, as the migrating birds begin
to flutter down from Europe, I like to take my gun
and climb across my mountain in the night, to lie
among the rocks, to watch the sky, to listen and wait
for the quail- and dove-filled dawn. The breeze fades
with moonset. A deep quiet sets in. There are only

3

the dull and subtle rhythms of suspense, the eternal lapping of the waves below, cool, dank smells.

The stars flicker. An antiphony of soft sounds is swallowed in the darkness. One finds oneself staring peacefully at the eternal. Here, in this splendid Greek night, we open secret doors into our souls.

Every morning, the same timid sough announces again the imminence of dawn. A gray light creeps behind the early-morning wind. The doves form up behind their leader cranes and, whirring among the treetops, take off in echelon after V-shaped echelon, fleeing southward toward Crete and Africa in their desperate search to escape death's septentrional threat.

Suddenly the sun appears in silent grandeur. It slips up over Hydra, over Poros, over Aegina, over Salamis and over the distant Marmora and Euxine seas, turning the still Aegean water into the colors of a peacock's tail. The sun's red shadow runs like flame across the tranquil surface of the water and life begins to dance along its fire path. In the sea, in the sky and on the land around us life resumes.

At first there is a threnody of songbirds bemoaning the dangers of the day; they rise, they rise. And then the entire compact island stirs itself alive. There is the braying of donkeys, the frisking of dolphins, the scurrying of cats, the crowing of cocks, the creaking of oarlocks, the rattling of shutters, the whistling of pigeons, the rumbling of anchor chains, the buzzing of flies, the scuffling of boots, the cropping of goats,

the chuckling of babies, the tolling of bells, the hollering of peddlers, the pecking of chickens, the shouting
of fishermen, the muttering of crones, the crackling of
cartwheels and the galloping of children. The hot sap
mounts beneath the sun and the fragrance of cycla-
men, of tansy, of thyme and of piny trees disseminates
about the island.

Here the impassive, diurnal contrast between light
and dark, life and death, is cozily expressed. Here one
is pushed by simplicity toward truth.

When one lies upon a mountaintop in Greece, one's
mind drawn up into the Eastern Mediterranean sky,
one knows why so many gods were cradled in these
seas, among these stones. For here, when one regards
the subject vertically, one grasps the infinity of distance
and the eternity of time. And death is the brother of
eternity; religion the search to flee it.

"That day [saith Hierome] I tremble as often as I
think of it. The terrible meditation of hell-fire, and
eternal punishment, much torments a sinful silly soul.
What's a thousand years to eternity? There mourning,
tears, eternal sorrow; death undying, and without
end. . . ."

So writes the melancholic Robert Burton, conclud-
ing with a quotation from Drexelius:

Eternity, that word, that tremendous word,
More threatening than all the artillery of heaven—
Eternity, that word, without end or beginning . . .

All who ever dwelled among these inland seas have
thought these thoughts. Even the happy Ovid wrote:

"Our life is short and tedious, and in the death of a man there is no recovery . . . and we shall be hereafter as though we had never been. . . ."

Thirty-six centuries ago Inanna, the Sumerian goddess of love, wandered beneath the horned Mediterranean moon bemoaning death, the loss of her people, her cities and her temples: "Oh, her heart! Oh her heart! Lo! Lo! Oh her heart! . . . The princess, her heart cries out in tears, Her heart cries out in tears and wails."

The Egyptians saw death above them in the night: "He that flieth flieth! He flieth away from you, ye men. He is no longer on earth, he is in the sky. . . . He rusheth at the sky as a heron, he hath kissed the sky as a hawk, he hath leapt skyward as a grasshopper. . . . If thou callest burial to mind, it is sadness, it is the bringing of tears, it is making a man sorrowful, it is hailing a man from his house and casting him upon the hill. Never wilt thou go forth again to behold the sun. . . . Death is before me today as the odour of myrrh . . . Death is before me today as the odour of lotus flowers. . . . Say not: 'I am too young for thee to carry off,' for thou knowest not thy death. Death cometh and leadeth away the babe that is still in the bosom of its mother, even as the man when he hath become old."

The frightened Egyptians passed through black passages and pillared halls seeking to placate death with humble declarations: "I have not done the abominable thing. I have not done the abomination of the Gods. . . . I have not caused pain. I have not caused hunger. I have not caused weeping. I have not slain, I have not commanded slaughter. I have not afflicted anyone. I have not baited for fish with dead fish." And death, embalmed death, came to them.

The kings of Babylon attempted to cheat death. During their festival of Sacaea, a five-day holiday begun on the sixteenth of the month of Lous, servants were given the places of their masters. A condemned prisoner, bearing the title of Zoganes, was dressed in the royal robes and seated upon the throne. And when his five-day rule was over, he was stripped of his finery, scourged and impaled to safeguard his monarch for yet another year. But death prevailed even over the mighty Babylonian kings.

The Hebrews inherited from primitive societies of the Mediterranean hinterland a harsh respect for death. Early they knew this to be synonymous with eternity. In the gospel that became Ecclesiastes they warned that out of nothing came man and thence he would return: "Vanity of vanities, saith the Preacher, vanity of vanities; all is vanity. What profit hath a man of all his labour which he taketh under the sun? One generation passeth away, and another generation cometh: but the earth abideth for ever. . . ." Man and beast, "All go unto one place; all are of the dust, and all turn to dust again."

The earliest Greeks, both Cretans with their horse-head helmets and savage blond Achaeans who murdered their way down from the North, shared this

gloomy acceptance. Pausanias complained: Where
are Troy, Persepolis, Cyzicus, Sparta, Argos and all
those famous ancient cities established by wandering
Greek enterprise? Where are Syracuse and Agrigen-
tum? What has become of Hiero and Empedocles of
such renown?

Burton comments sadly: ". . . cities, men, monu-
ments decay, nor can its fabrick preserve the solid
globe; the names are only left, those at length for-
gotten, and are involved in perpetual night. . . ."

The life-loving and fantastically active Greeks con-
soled themselves by giving kinetic energy to death.
They conceived of two dim limbos, one happily inhabited by gods and their human relatives, the other
by shades and furies deep in a moated, dog-protected
cavern on the mainland west of Spetsais. And not
only did they try to endow themselves with immortality by calling their gods kinsmen; but they made
these gods men to the point of dying. Until early in the
Christian era the grave of Zeus was shown to visitors
in Crete.

Pericles revered an honorable death and Socrates
knew approximately what death was. These two great
men of antiquity joined in respecting the inevitable.
When the cypress coffins of those who had fallen in
the Spartan war were borne to the Beautiful suburb
of Athens to be laid within the public cenotaph,
Pericles pronounced what Thucydides calls "an ap-
propriate panegyric." The slain heroes, he told the
Athenian tribes, had earned fame by their means of

dying. Dying rather than death was important to Pericles. Man could not control death but he could find it proudly.

Heroes, Pericles said, "have the whole earth for their tomb; and in lands far from their own . . . there is enshrined in every breast a record unwritten with no tablet to preserve it, except that of the heart."

Nobody can now pretend to know where Pericles or his soldiers are buried other than in our hearts. Nor are there any concrete traces left of Socrates although, when I first came to Greece, there rotted on the Athenian outskirts a memorable olive stump, sinewy, pocked with rotten holes, almost as broad as it was tall, still bearing every spring a few green leaves much as the whiskers sprout upon a corpse. This, as legend had it, was the tree beneath which Socrates walked with Plato, speaking of death and the eternal.

Socrates feared nothing and death least of all. He compared man's way of meeting destiny with that of the trumpeting swan. "Will you not allow that I have as much of the spirit of prophecy in me as the swans?" he asked his friend Simmias. "For they, when they perceive that they must die, having sung all their life long, do then sing more lustily than ever, rejoicing in the thought that they are about to go away to the god whose ministers they are. But men, because they are themselves afraid of death, slanderously affirm of the swans that they sing a lament at the last, not considering that no bird sings when cold, or hungry, or in pain. . . . I . . . would not go out of life less merrily than the swans."

By exposing hypocrisy and deception, Socrates was an infernal nuisance while he lived. His kindest act was showing men how to die. He left to them a hope that perhaps death held in store something more cheerful than permanent extinction. He believed otherwise himself; but he saw in hope a crutch that could support the weak across the final threshold. His own death, as recounted by Phaedo, was the grandest gift he could bequeath a generation he had taught to doubt.

The ugly, benevolent old cynic, condemned for upsetting the orderly patterns of a society that needed order to survive, was fascinated by the process of his own dying. He folded his robe about him, lay upon his prison bed, almost merrily drank down the poison cup of hemlock and described the effects to his friends.

Plato was ill when his master accepted fate. But fifteen other disciples of the philosopher watched that master die. When Socrates' chains were removed on the day he was to drink the poison, his wife, Xanthippe, was led out wailing and beating herself as he sat rubbing his legs to restore the circulation. Socrates comforted his friends, arguing: "I ought to be grieved at death, if I were not persuaded in the first place that I am going to other gods who are wise and good (of which I am as certain as I can be of any such matters), and secondly (though I am not so sure of this last) to men departed, better than those whom I leave behind; and therefore I do not grieve as I might have done, for I have good hope that there is yet something remaining for the dead. . . ."

Here he was interrupted by Crito, who reminded him that the jailer charged with executing the sentence had cautioned the philosopher not to talk too much before taking the draught. That would "interfere with the action of the poison; persons who excite themselves are sometimes obliged to take a second or even a third dose." This did not impress Socrates, who valued fine dying. He said: "Let him mind his business and be prepared to give the poison twice or even thrice if necessary."

He accordingly resumed: "I desire to prove to you that the real philosopher has reason to be of good cheer when he is about to die. . . . For I deem that the true victory of philosophy is likely to be misunderstood by other men; they do not perceive that he [the philosopher] is always pursuing death and dying; and if this be so, and he has had the desire for death all his life long, why when his time comes should he repine at that which he had been always pursuing and desiring?"

Socrates took a bath so that, prior to his funeral, "the women may not have the trouble of washing my body after I am dead." Then, at sunset, he accepted the cup of poison. The jailer instructed him: "You have only to walk around until your legs are heavy, and then to lie down, and the poison will act." Socrates drank; and his friends burst into tears. He berated them, saying: "I sent the women away mainly in order that they might not misbehave in this way, for I have been told that a man should die in peace."

He walked about until his legs failed and he began to lose all feeling in them. Later he lay down and said: "When the poison reaches the heart, that will be the end." Soon after that he grew cold about the groin. He had covered his face but suddenly uncovered it and said: "Crito, I owe a cock to Asclepius; will you remember to pay the debt?" These were his last words. He, who knew what life's meaning was, also knew the meaning of death. But this he did not tell his friends. He did not wish to frighten them.

Death in the Mediterranean is perhaps particularly sad, for life is so important and agreeable upon this sea. Always, Mediterranean men have sought to assume the task of divinity by giving everything its life and name. They peopled stars and constellations with heroes or the beasts of fancy: myth figures: mermaids, selkies, centaurs, lapiths, minotaurs, swan maidens, nymphs and paranymphs, goat pans, goat giants, crow titans, chimaeras, harpies, gorgons, sphinxes, satyrs—the cleft-footed, furry-hocked, feather-winged, serpent-toothed, tuft-tailed, antelope-horned, bull-chested, ram-flanked, stallion-slung, seal-flippered creatures that haunt this area's life and dreamed-of after-life.

From one end of the wise sea to the other, men have spoken of life and thought of death, have danced for life and sung of death, danced their horas and their kolos, sung their dirges, fadoes, monodies and lamentations, blowing upon conch shells, sheep horns, bronze trumpets and the twin-piped flute, strumming lyres, guslas and one-stringed rubabas. They have sought to cheat death by making of death a living thing. For the Manichaeans, as for the later Serbs upon the Adriatic, death came as a flapping bird, an ill-omened raven flying in at dawn. The birds of death were black birds, grievously singing kar, kar, kar as they fluttered down upon the wind-bitten crags, the swift rivers and the seas.

Death here is a familiar. It is honored by church-bells in an olive grove and the agonizing shriek of donkeys stumbling over pretty-patterned cobbles to the graveyard. Death is a mad shepherd's flute, calling ceaselessly.

The peoples of this sea land have always accustomed themselves to death and tried to elude its implications: the Egyptian monotheists, the Assyrian Baalists, the Molochites, the Achaean and Balearic worshipers of the Great Mother, the animists, the deists, the Yezidi, kowtowing to the devil; the Hebrews, the Moslems, each venerating chosen gods. Where Jewish and Greek thinking first collided, Christianity developed with its comforting doctrine of resurrection and salvation. But, in the end, all turn backward and inward upon themselves, for "All go unto one place; all are of the dust, and all turn to dust again."

Those words must have been conceived at night and composed in cold darkness. For they are the pure

13

words of death. It is only at night, alone on a hard mountain, that death assumes its proper, solitary grandeur. For this, among life's experiences, is one we cannot share.

Psychologists claim they can probe the deep hidden mysteries of birth and the womb. But we cannot partake of death with others; only, at best, our dying. When Gertrude Stein was on her bed of death she turned to those around her and she asked: "What is the answer?" Hearing no reply, she then asked: "If so, what is the question?"

And why is the question necessary? Why must we understand that which by its essence is not to be understood? This aspiration is the supreme vanity, indeed the divine vanity. Craving for reason and explanation is a phenomenon invented by ourselves in order to make ourselves suffer. It requires no answer —save from and by ourselves.

And the answers we give one another are those we cannot comprehend: reincarnation, transubstantiation, immortality and intricate patterns of time.

The answers are a presumption—but the question is an impertinence. Nevertheless, the problem has always tormented theologians. Some, like the Greeks, taught that in the beginning there was chaos, that from this the gods and their assistants made what we now call order. Some, like the Jews, taught that in the beginning there was nothing, and that God created. Both, by presupposing an eternal life before, whether material or divine, prepared for the syllogistic argument of eternal afterlife. But neither, in the end, succeeded in eliminating death and its supreme dolor.

Nor did any of the great religions of the antique world. All they could teach was an *ethos* for living. "You and the Lord," said the priest to the peasant, "have worked well here." Said the peasant to the priest: "Yes. You should have seen the place when the Lord had it to himself."

All around us, in the daytime, there is striving life. The wine presses groan; foam covers their great bellies; a drizzle of wine fills the vat. But entombed in distant Mongolia lie thousands of dinosaurs surrounded by sterile eggs. And here, across the way, in Epidaurus, in Mycenae, can the hero climb from his beehive tomb?

He can never arise. Nor can the plump Theban, with his succulent brain and flaccid neck; nor that oval-headed Sicilian genius, nor the puffy old Turk in his bath of steam surrounded by nodding Osmanli eunuchs, nor the miserable fellah mother who pricked out one eye of her man child with a rusty needle to preserve (from Mohammed Ali's draft) his traction power for a wooden plow. Nor any of the innumerable generations embalmed with such delicate science that they would not stink in death. Dead kulak, muzhik, Jew, Catholic, Communist, liberal, lord, serf, slave, sonar technician, maker of mobiles, pugilist, intellectual, dung-clotted peasant; world conqueror; young men and young women whose hair still smells of marigolds; where are those naked fellows, their souls?

Even today, as in old Egypt, the hot cat whines and drags her rump, tweaked by the land tides of the moon. In rockets, as in Noah's ark, the animals are screaming, Let me out, Let me out. The Hebrew millennium and the Christian resurrection deceive them.

The killers and the killed are gone together: Ares Velouchiotis, that bitter-brave Greek partisan leader of the Second World War, who ordered his youthful band of sadists to stand about with steel whips and see him suck blood; Pavle Dokić, the very last hajduk, who strode through the mountains of the Homolje like a wolf; Ibn Saud, the cunning old king, who sat by Fatima's well watching the first breeze of evening stir the palm fronds, watching the foxes and lapwings and desert rats and fingering his wounds; and the Yemeni Imam, stooping and pondering his hennaed feet, while drifting down from the Baluchi coast came sambuks loaded with stolen slaves and dates. The crones, fragrant of fruit or stinking of decrepitude, scented with lavender, pine, ambergris and musk, dressed in black Chantilly lace and drinking the black wine of Málaga beneath a red sky; the people who have known pain and labor, the rain and the wind in the fields; the queens who rustled by in a slight breeeze, followed by the aura of their perfume; Shayama, with her untied tresses dangling, the bells of her anklets jingling and bees humming above her crimson feet: all are together with the dodo and the mastodon and none has avoided death.

We would all outwit this death, no matter how miserable our lot. In Bohemia the brutalized peasants used to carry death's figure to a high rock and heave it into a pond while singing: "Death swims on the water, summer will soon be here, we carried Death away for you, we brought the summer." Or they chanted: "We have carried away Death and brought Life back"; and then they would burn death's straw figure. But death triumphed even there.

Men fear death because they refuse to understand it. But the manner of death is more important than death itself. Fine dying is man's privilege, for that man can himself control. We cannot influence death but we can influence the style of our departure. Men surprise themselves by the fashion in which they face this death: some more proudly and more valiantly than ever they dared imagine; and some in abject terror.

In the pre-dawn stillness, the birds begin to stir. The birds are both life and death, borne by the winds they know and cannot control, the lively doves and the bleak, cawing crows.

Do the birds on their way to equatorial resurrection ponder what it is they flee? What do they know of the sweet and sour schools of death as hunters emerge from beneath trees and bang into the early-morning air? Can they contemplate how they die as they tumble, bloodied, into thickets? They cannot even manage their dying, much less their living. They cannot muster that pitiful final flash of dignity we like to associate with man.

How many of us live and die like birds, not knowing where we are bound, why and whence we came? Draža Mihajlović, the Serbian guerrilla, said before he faced his enemies' firing squad: "I found myself in a whirl of events and intrigues. I found myself in a whirl of events and strivings. . . . Destiny was merciless towards me when it threw me into the most difficult whirlwinds. I wanted much, I began much, but the whirlwind, the world whirlwind, carried me and my work away."

And now, on my mountain, as the stars fall out of sight, there is the first rustle of awakening quail. There is the scuttling of doves, and pigeons are pouring from their sea caves. Leaden clouds lumber like whales before the sun and the salt-sweat, garlic-tasting day begins.

Southward in time and space the Egyptians chanted: "Beautiful is thine appearing in the horizon of heaven, thou living sun, the first who lived! Thou risest in the eastern horizon, and fillest every land with thy beauty. . . . The birds fly out of their nests and their wings praise thy *ka*. All wild beasts dance on their feet, all that fly and flutter—they live when thou arisest for them. . . . The fishes leap up before thy face. Thy rays are in the sea."

Is this the morning? Are those birds? Their voices are everywhere?

TWO

The Implications of Death

WITH ALL OUR pretensions to knowledge, mankind has never properly identified the difference between existence and nonexistence, the translation of life to death. What we proudly hail as life is but the result of solar energy that, flowing for perhaps five billion years, produced on our little planet certain biological phenomena and what we call intelligence. The sun itself, a condensation of dust and gas, might well have had a different history. In that case the vanity of this book would not be.

A sun must shine interminably long and steadily, spawning planets and attracting them into stable orbits of sufficient warmth to initiate, from random mutations, tides and winds, the beasts and organisms we fondly deem rational. Where else, we wonder with our special pride, where else in the vast universe has this phenomenon been achieved? Are we the only thinking creatures who, for example, can imagine God?

We do not know. Our celestial explorations still are far too shallow.

Alpha Centauri, the nearest other sun of which we are aware, remains 4.3 light years away. One light year is 5,880,000,000,000 miles. What beings could live long enough to travel this huge distance and survive? To get to Tau Ceti, another sun, separated from our planet by merely 10.8 light years, would require hundreds of thousands of years of travel, even at the dizzy speed of earth-launched rockets.

We have come from nonexistence, in terms of the only meaning our mental dictionaries comprehend, across unlimited spans of time and space. And when we regard the distant stars it is hard to conceive how many have long since vanished in explosions while we wait for that information to arrive at about 186,000 miles a second, the speed of light.

Life to us is an egoistic concept and death difficult to define because we do not precisely know its nature. What is death to the tobacco mosaic virus, to lichen, to man? Can it be described in all-inclusive yet intelligible terms? A corpse may cease to function normally—and yet, as it is shoved into the ground or brilliantly incinerated, is it not crammed with living cells whose persevering energy we choose to disregard?

We prefer to ignore this perplexing thought because our dominating organs would by then no longer function (although the Caribbean zombie, a soulless resurrection in a moving body, remains a curious fancy of that paradox, living death).

Human death is legally cessation of the heartbeat as heard by auscultation. But even today medicine can violate the law; for, time after time, the dead are revived by cardiac massage and oxygen inhalation. If this succeeds within five minutes, renascence is accomplished. Our most sensitive part, the brain, can yet survive undamaged. Thus, in truth the law is wrong.

In an irretrievable sense, the brain dies first, and only then the heart, the kidneys and the liver. A leg can be what we term dead for two whole hours, tied off from the rest of a complicated body; yet it will function again if still attached to a working brain and heart. So even death is in its early stages but a matter of degree. Time alone makes it absolute.

It is this aspect of time, infinite time, that brings to death associated terror. If only it were but a long, long sleep! How one craves the assurance of return, even a millennium hence! Is death less permanent because we can still regard, along the sacred Eleusis road in Greece, the living stump of an olive tree beneath which Plato walked?

Death is the only one of life's experiences we cannot share. No one save the mystic claims or dares to probe the mystery of death; nor can we impart to others what its lessons truly are, how it feels and is. The only lesson we can pass on to our fellows is the example of living decently and dying well.

Plato quotes Socrates as saying: "In reality, then, Simmias, those who pursue philosophy rightly study to die; and to them of all men death is least formidable." The first among sages speaks this way of the death process: The soul "is separated in a pure state, taking nothing of the body with it, but having shunned it and gathered itself within itself, as constantly studying this; but this is nothing else than to pursue philosophy aright, and in reality to study how to die easily; would not this be to study how to die?"

The ultimate Socratic theory, as profound in our age of exploding science as in the age of peripatetic thought, is simply: "Indeed I should not be surprised if Euripedes speaks the truth when he says, 'And who knows if to live be but to die, to die to live?' And I dare say in reality we are all dead. Some time ago I heard a certain philosopher say that we are even now dead, and that our body is our tomb."

Emotionless Aristotle introduced impurity into this pattern of thought. He confused the substance of philosophical reality with the shadow of what purported to be technical knowledge, a fault that has persisted ever since. He argued as follows: "Every member and the entire animal body possess to a certain degree congenital heat. Consequently we see that during life animals are warm [which could scarcely apply to fish or snakes or roaches] but when dead and deprived of life they are cold. The source of this heat in sanguineous animals must be sought in the heart, and in the bloodless animals in the analagous organ. . . . Consequently, all the other parts of the body may become cold and yet life may continue, but when the master-organ becomes cold, life is destroyed entirely, because this is the source of heat for distribution to all other organs. . . . Life, then, must go hand in hand with the continuance of this heat, and what we call death is its discontinuance. . . . One must understand that an animal is by nature moist and warm, whereas old age is dry and cold, and so is death."

The Greek philosophers examined death with fascination. Heraclitus and Empedocles reasoned that death was a changing element of life. Empedocles concluded by discounting categorically all notions of immortality. "And I shall tell thee another thing," he said. "There is no coming into being of aught that perishes, nor any end of it in baneful death; but only mingling and change of what has been mingled. Coming into being is but a name given to these by men." In other words, there is no true distinction between life and death, descriptive terms invented by human conceit for, if nothing else, purposes of convenience.

Said Empedocles: "When the elements have been mingled in the fashion of a man and come to the light of day, or in the fashion of the race of wild beasts and plants or birds, then men say that these came into being; and when they are separated, they call that woeful death. They call it not aright; but I too follow the custom, and call it so myself."

Lucretius was the poetic Roman spokesman for Greece's Epicurean school. He approached death from the viewpoint of the modern atomic scientist. He too entertained no hopes of immortality. Furthermore, he discerned: "By protracting life we do not deduct one jot from the time when death shall last. . . . Nay, you may live to complete as many generations as you will, nevertheless that everlasting death will still be waiting. . . ." And he "who has made an end of life with to-day's sun" shall be dead no less a time "than he who fell many a month and year before." You will be dead as long as Adam.

Lucretius avoided the later and greater illusion that there must needs be a beginning and an end and that, consequently, divinity both precedes and follows what we know as time.

"No single thing returns to nothing," Lucretius taught, "but all at their disruption return to the elements of matter. . . . [They] do not utterly pass away that seem to do, since Nature makes up again one thing from another, and suffers not one to be born unless aided by another's death." But, he added, "whatever by being changed passes outside its own boundaries, at once this is the death of that which was before."

He saw that our frightened struggle to claim eternal life was doomed and foolish, and his was the cool, indifferent forecast of a cool, indifferent future: "For if by chance anyone is to have misery and pain in the future, he must needs himself also exist then in that time to be miserable. Since death takes away this possibility, and forbids him to exist for whom these inconveniences may be gathered together, we may be sure that there is nothing to be feared after death, that he who is not cannot be miserable. . . ."

The lucid logic of the Greeks and their Roman students, in which faith in divinity was relegated to a minor, pleasant, choral role, has been discarded by religions we have come to know as modern. Today, most organized religion recognizes that there is no fear of sleep when there is confidence in awakening. Therefore it offers unwarranted faith as a substitute for reason, a promise of a future in order to control man's present. The equation is unbalanced. Mysticism is the key.

The soldiers saw Jesus "was dead already" on the cross and "they broke not his legs"; but to the initiates he lived as the son of God. And from this touching belief St. John the Divine concocted his celestial theater based on the numerology of seven and painted a verbal rainbow for his followers in the seven churches of Asia: bejeweled thrones, jasper, sardine stone, emeralds; white-clad elders wearing golden crowns; thunder, lightning, burning fire lamps; beasts like lions, calves, eagles murmuring of holiness, seven-horned, seven-eyed lambs; seven-headed sea creatures, wine-drinking angels; fire, brimstone; cinnamon, frankincense, ointments, fine flour; harpers, musicians,

27

pipers, trumpeters—all the terrifying and lovely things imaginable to the tenants of this earth, warning them of the eternal price of faithlessness and offering them the eternal reward of loyalty to what they could not possibly understand: a beautiful, frightening vision of confusion.

Islam, which together with Judaism and Christianity forms the Western family of religions, embellished a similar credo. It pledged the most gaudy of eternities to its adherents in exchange for loyal devotion during this transitory life.

Like that of the Apocalypse, the Moslem paradise is strangely influenced by multiples of seven. There are seven heavens and the excellent steed, Alborak, who bore Mohammed to these places, was furnished with seventy brace of wings. One angel in the seventh heaven had seventy thousand heads, in each of which were seventy thousand tongues. Each tongue in turn could speak at once with seventy thousand voices. And Allah, Himself, the great God, hid his face behind seventy thousand veils. The glory of abode replete with precious stones, music, maidens and above all that desert rarity, water, was as assured to Mohammed's followers as to the Prophet when, as the delayed victim of a poison plot in Khaibar, he died at the age of sixty-one. He is now scheduled, after failing to return to this earth following one millennium, to make his presence known again in A.D. 2632.

Islam was infected by Oriental influences, unlike

Christianity, which moved through Greece and Rome. It developed an interesting form in the Sufism of Khorasan, athwart the trade routes leading into India. That divergence, which spread into various dervish sects, taught that dying came within the individual and living came as part of God. This would seem to be a link more with the old Persian dogmas of Zoroaster than with Mediteranean thought.

Zoroaster pledged salvation in death to those who had adequately propitiated Ahura-Mazda, god of Good and Light. The saved were told that the soul (*ruvan*) would not be conscious of any suffering while the body (*tan*) resolved into its basic elements; the corpse itself would be inert, unmoving and devoid of feeling; the soul, on the contrary, retaining the delightful attribute of intellectual awareness and perceiving its heavenly destination, would be filled with joy as it entered the Best Existence possible. A final promise was eventual resurrection in which body and soul would rejoin each other. The wicked, on the other hand, were doomed to darkness, shrieking as they went the Wail of Woe. "The fate of each man is determined in strict accordance with the kind of life he has led on earth, or 'the first life.' " But, in one or another form, Zoroastrianism holds death will be cheated by happy or unhappy eternal consciousness.

The further east one goes, the less specific is the religious pledge of afterlife, perhaps because Asian existence has rarely been happy enough to stimulate desire for its repetition. The lesson of Confucius, who preached veneration of the dead, is confusing. It suits neither logic nor its antithesis, inflamed mysticism with assurance of material comfort or discomfort.

The Master taught: "All who live, must die and, dying, return to the earth. . . . The bones and flesh moulder below and, hidden away, become the earth of the fields. But the spirit issues forth and is displayed on high in a condition of glorious brightness."

Blessed Buddha said to his admirers: "Bhikshus, never forget it: decay is inherent in all component things." And when he expired with this wise observation the mighty earth was shaken, thunderbolts fell and such gods as inhabited the sky (for Buddhism teaches that there is no Supreme Being) did shriek with the sound of drums.

Buddhism, as evolved by its Zen sect, has produced a tranquil and purely philosophical concept of death. This is well described by a German adherent: "Like the beginner the swordsmaster is fearless, but, unlike him, he grows daily less and less accessible to fear. Years of unceasing meditation have taught him that life and death are at bottom the same and belong to the same stratum of fact. He no longer knows what fear of life and terror of death are. He lives—and this is thoroughly characteristic of Zen—happily enough in the world, but ready at any time to quit it without being in the least disturbed by the thought of death.

"To be free from the fear of death," the adherent warns, "does not mean pretending to oneself, in one's good hours, that one will not tremble in the face of death, and that there is nothing to fear. Rather, he who masters both life and death is free from fear of any kind to the extent that he is no longer capable of experiencing what fear feels like."

During the seventeenth century an aristocratic soldier of the Japanese Shogun told his Zen fencing teacher: "There is one thing of which I can say I am complete master. When I was still a boy, the thought came upon me that as a Samurai I ought in no circumstances to be afraid of death, and I have grappled with the problem of death now for some years, and finally the problem of death ceased to worry me." This confession evoked admiration from the Zen instructor. "The ultimate secrets of swordsmanship," he commented, "also lie in being released from the thought of death."

The harsh landscape of the Middle East inspired the great Western faiths of Judaism, Christianity and Islam with their insistence on stern goodness in this world and their promise of joy hereafter. The mountains and jungles of the Orient evolved a different, more chaotic theology. But pure and concentrated thinking on the great problem of death arrived, by tortuous means, at similar ends among the philosophers of Buddhism and of ancient Athens. The lesson, in the end, was that life and death were the same; the former should be well lived and the latter tranquilly ignored.

Because death is the most powerful stimulant toward hope of God—a hope that promises immortal

benefits to those who rely on what they don't believe
—most of the later philosophers in the Occident have
been deeply tinged by religious thought. Descartes
sought to resolve his own bewilderment with that
curiously perfect French logic which so often termi-
nates in paradox. By a process of neat reasoning, he
concluded that "the mind, so far as it can be known
by aid of a natural philosophy, is immortal."

Despite this, Descartes remained preoccupied with
death. He worked hard to produce what he called his
"fruits," so that they might remain upon Life's tree
after he had departed. And he cheerfully wrote a
friend: "As to death, of which you warn me, although
I know well that it can, at any moment take me, I
feel to this time, thanks to God, teeth sound enough,
and strong, that I do not have to worry about that for
thirty years or so, if it does not come unannounced."
In fact, he labored placidly on for eleven years, never
quite sure, despite his protestations, of just what
would await his "immortality" of the mind.

Spinoza, profoundly involved in circuitous meta-
physics, ended with the conclusion that the world and
God were one, in reality, and God the substance of all
things. Individuals merely formed aspects, or acci-
dents, of that substance. Spinoza defined death as
follows: "I consider that a body undergoes death,
when the proportion of motion and rest which obtained mutually among its several parts is changed."
However, while appearing to equate "motion" with
what more poetic thinkers call "soul," he had stern

words for those who lived morally solely to escape damnation: "He who is led by fear, and does good in order to escape evil, is not led by reason." And he ended up, a Dutch Jew, with the same final thoughts as the Athenian Socrates and the Buddhist monk Jetsun Milarepa: "A free man thinks of death least of all things; and wisdom is a meditation not of death but of life."

Bishop Berkeley tended to view both life and death as dreams, as "passive ideas in the mind." His conclusion was more doubting and more optimistic than that of many other seventeenth-century meditators. "I see no difficulty in conceiving a change of state, such as is vulgarly called Death," he conceded, "as well without as with material substance. It is sufficient for that purpose that we allow sensible bodies; the existence of which I am . . . far from questioning (as philosophers are used to do). . . . Now, it seems very easy to conceive the *soul* to exist in a separate state . . . and to exercise herself on new ideas, without the intervention of those tangible things we call our bodies. It is even very possible to conceive how the soul may have ideas of color without an eye, or of sounds without an ear"—a very Zen-like conclusion.

Montesquieu was frankly bewildered by death's prospect. On the one hand he admitted: "A great thinker assures me that I shall die as an insect. He seeks to impress on me that I am but a modification of matter. . . . According to him I am not a being distinguished from any other being; he lifts from me

33

all that which I held to be most personal. . . . Why seek glory? Why feel shame? . . . I am inclined to believe in this philosopher." But, on the other hand, he said with querulous hope: "When belief in the immortality of the soul is proved to be an error, I will be very sorry to deny my own belief. I do not understand atheism; I assure you that I am not as humble as are the atheists."

For Rousseau "Death is the cure of all evils you bring upon yourself; nature would not have you suffer perpetually . . . the more we seek to escape from it, the more we are aware of it; and we go through life in the fear of death, blaming nature for the evils we have inflicted on ourselves by our neglect of her laws." He offered this sensible advice: "We enter into the lists at birth, we leave them at death. Of what avail is it to learn how well to conduct one's chariot when one is at the end of the course? There is nothing more to consider, then, on the manner of one's leaving it."

Voltaire, who was influenced by the Roman Stoics, quoted Epictetus as showing us the way to die: "You wish that I leave this magnificent spectacle, I leave it; and I thank You a thousand times over that You have deigned to admit me there where I can see Your works manifested and to see before my eyes the order with which You govern this universe." But Voltaire's sense of humor could not allow him to avoid expressions of scorn for those who feared his negative conclusions.

"When I am asked if after my death my senses will

remain intact," he quipped, "I am almost inclined to ask in turn if the song of a rossignol remains after the bird has been devoured by an eagle." He defied the foundations of Cartesian teaching and he wrote: "The hope of existing after death is established on the love of self during life; it is founded on the probability that what thinks *will* think. No proof exists of this point, because a thing proven is a thing of which the contrary is a contradiction, and because there have never been disputes on demonstrated truths." He mocked "revealed" truth and listed the innumerable crimes man has committed in its name.

Sigmund Freud, whose thinking has such strong influence in our time, was affected both by the ancient Greeks and Schopenhauer. Freud agreed with the latter that death is the "true result and to that extent the purpose of life." Summarizing his own theory of the death instinct, the founder of psychoanalysis said: "The upshot of our enquiry so far has been the drawing of a sharp distinction between the 'ego instincts' and the sexual instincts, and the view that the former exercise a thrust towards death and the latter towards a prolongation of life."

It is curious to apply Freud's own methods of analysis to Freud himself. For once he said he thought of death every day of his life. After a fainting spell in 1912, when he regained consciousness his first remark was: "How sweet it must be to die."

And John Dewey, who lost two children in their youth, although he lived to be ninety-three never recovered from that tragic shock. He tried calmly if unsatisfactorily to discern a contrast between life and death and to ascertain the latter's implications. God, for him, was almost an excuse, a crutch: "There are so many people who would feel bewildered if not hurt were they denied the intellectual right to use the term 'God.'" And everything was indecisive, both life and death, neither of which could properly be defined even with Berkeley's dreamy confidence. "Living . . . is not something which goes on below the skin-surface of an organism: it is always an inclusive affair involving connection, interaction of what is within the organic body and what lies outside in space and time, and with higher organisms far outside." A broken connection, like Spinoza's loss of motion, is death.

The Existentialists, more clever than profound, derived from the essential principles of Kant and Nietzsche. With immense practicality they teach that our destiny as creatures is limited by death and therefore we must decide to be nothing more than we already are, to live in this absurd world and resign ourselves to a finish of that experience.

Kierkegaard, the founder of this doubting school, dismissed the presumptuous legend of Descartes. He wrote: "'I think, therefore I am,' does not conform to the reality of man's existence because the less I think, the more I am, and vice versa." Kafka sees death's door as an individual portal each man can open only for himself, finding his own combination to the lock. And Heidegger insists that man's job is simply to accept existence for what it is, an existence opposite to death. Sartre is gloomy. He reasons there can be no individual essence of the individual until his death, because essence is something which applies to what no longer is. And, with sad wisdom, he admits: "Even if I think it is God that I obey, it is I who decided that it was God who spoke to me."

Abstract philosophy is intimately linked to religion. Each, in the end, impinges upon life and death; each guides the living and counsels in the art of dying. All philosophers belong in Heaven, if only they could get there.

As a young man, before the last Great War, I spent many hours discussing life and death in the Albanian *tekke*, or monastery, of the Grand Baba of the Bektashi, a somewhat eccentric Moslem sect. These delightfully original priests had once been chaplains to the Ottoman Janissaries, that splendid fighting force made up of boys taken out of Christian families and trained to battle for the Sultan and Islam. The soldiers and their monkish brothers conspired too often against the Sublime Porte itself so, in the nineteenth century, the Janissaries were banned and the Bektashi were banished with their kettledrums, outmoded gear and highly heretical thoughts to the little province on the Adriatic. There I used to meet with the brothers near craggy Kruja village, sitting on cushions in a wide circle of the brethren, beside the Grand Baba himself, a handsome, bearded ancient.

The Abbot (fingering his crenelated white brimless top hat and playing with the large crystal ball suspended from his belt): "Death is but transmogrification. No one can see through the other side of the mirror, my pupil."

The Pupil: "And of those who teach us what death is, who among them tells the truth?"

The Abbot: "None among them, pupil. For none among them knows—or even suspects."

At this point, and always, one of the brethren passed the decanter of fiery arrack, ignoring Koranic proscriptions on alcohol; and we drank.

The Abbot: "Here, in these fumes, we find pleasure and temporary solace. It helps us to remember in our ease that there is good in all who believe in good, regardless of their faith or lack of it. Tolerance is what is important. And death, as a brother, comes to embrace all men."

Outside, among the rocks and woods, the cuckoos sang. The horned moon of Skanderbeg slipped over the peaks. And the brethren passed from lips to lips the cooling hubble-bubble pipe, contemplating the approach of their unutterably gloomy relative, death.

How refreshing and how sad; what a far and hopeless cry from that stream of thinking, based on resurrection and untested promise, that courses through Western faiths from the time of the Sadducees, before Christ, and the Corinthians, before St. Paul.

The medieval Catholic scholars and the Buddhist bonzes argued pros and cons of celestially inspired mutations—without conclusion. Bodies change as particles are replaced by other particles and suffer time's deterioration. What body would be raised, the ancient or the young? Would a limbless man be reincarnated whole? In the Christian Heaven, can one expect to meet one's grandmother as a white-haired crone or as a fresh young virgin?

The Sadducees assumed only a body like man's present body would greet a resurrection. They posed to Jesus the problem: If a husband has outlived seven wives, which shall be his everlasting mate? And are the happy beasts around us resurrected? Would our eternal body be split up to restore the eternal bodies of the beasts we ate? Does a frog possess a soul?

In the end, most philosophers of Christendom, when driven by despair or intrepidity to answer these ultimate questions, fall back on the interpretations of the heathen Greeks: a thin species of immortality, intellectual, joyless ghosts.

Man is so touchingly egocentric he can conceive with neither willingness nor resignation the idea of immutable death as it impinges on himself. Even the Communists, who boast of atheism and claim to scorn death, if not defy it, try to cheat its ravages by stuffing their greatest heroes and placing them in lugubrious and massive mausoleums akin to the tombs of Nilotic Thebes.

In more than three thousand years of recorded thought we have not dented the surface of death's implications. For Socrates we are already dead, entombed within our bodies. For Aristotle death is the discontinuance of heat; for Heraclitus but a phase of constant change; for Lucretius death presents "all"; for the Zen teachers life and death are the same; for Spinoza death is an absence of motion; for Rousseau it is a cure of evils; for Schopenhauer it represents life's purpose.

During long, long generations we have thought of death with the icy logic that sprang from sea-washed Attica and with the purple-nighted mysticism of the Middle Eastern deserts, without beginning and without end in reason, confusing the intemperate past, the warm present and the unbearably cold future, stillness with motion, and proceeding through timeless time. Today we live, as we imagine, harder and more excitingly, and we think less of the abstractions that defeat us. We travel faster. We penetrate the first veneer of space. We seek, as it were, to escape death, like the flesh and the devil, by running away. And still we run, feverishly, into a limitless vacuum where death rules undisturbed.

THREE

The Halo of Death

SAINTS HAVE in common holiness and death; canonic formalities are never granted to a living candidate. Even Cao Dai, that curious Vietnamese sect which aspires to join Buddha, Lao-tse and Confucius to a Roman Catholic form of hierarchy, insists that death is a saintly precondition.

Cao Dai worships the human eye in its serpent-pillared, demon-painted, flower-carved cathedral at Tay Ninh. Just beneath the eye in rank are Nguyen Binh Khiem, an eccentric Indo-Chinese, Victor Hugo and the Chinese revolutionary Sun Yat-sen. Winston Churchill is a saint-elect, but only death will qualify him for full veneration by the conical-hatted priests marching to sound their red tocsin.

Sainthood is a laborious process for the Roman

Catholic Church, which requires virtual proof of miraculous gifts. Joan of Arc waited almost five centuries for the honor. But Greek Orthodoxy is less strict. A man or woman is simply considered a saint on "general recognition" of a holy life. Then the Holy Synod arranges liturgical changes to reverence newcomers where "entertain him all ye saints above in solemn troops and sweet societies."

Miracle-making saints are frequently shared in pieces. Their relics have high practical value and are often dismembered and scattered to the various altars of the faithful world. And Heaven is acknowledgedly filled with saints. There one can easily imagine a delicate, haloed company nodding to music by Mozart, Bach, Vivaldi; surrounded by Florentine angels of the *quattrocento*, probably dressed in the more fashionable *trecento* styles and walking on the soft flowering grass painted by the masters of Siena and Perugia.

There, of a shining night, one would listen to a new tone poem especially composed by Palestrina for the lute, the ram's horn shofar, the zither and the tortoiseshell harp designed to accompany David's own recitals.

The colors of Heaven are evidently milk white (the bluish white of thin, fat-free milk), that special green concocted by Bassano and remembered by El Greco; purple, pink, silver, gold and mother-of-pearl. Heaven smells of lilac, cinnamon, lilies-of-the-valley, orange blossoms, jasmine, tuberoses, Mediterranean salt air and, on feast days, garlic. Its sounds are fragile: the gurgling of small brooks, the leaping of fish, the lapping of puppies and the evening breeze amid the olive trees. The temperature is approximately 74° Fahrenheit. Most saints and angels eat Turkish delight, honey from Mount Hymettus bees (or their shades), black bread, manna, raisins, white goats' cheese, ham, lamb, jam and goose liver, and drink mead or a saffron, lightly resinated wine. They seem sexless, apart from those in the noisy, perfumed Moslem quarter ruled by benevolent and bearded Imams.

Amid these good people sits Mohammed, slightly sullen in expression as he contemplates his promised return to earth through the miracle of a man-mother. Around him are his most distinguished followers, headed by Fatima, Ali, the sherifs and the caliphs. Muezzins, their gray beards flowing in the brilliant air, lean over terraced, towering minarets and summon the merry faithful to prayer, interrupting the happy soldiers of the Prophet, perfumed, oiled and washed in scented soap, as they dandle plump ladies in patterned, geometric gardens, resting by the banks of purling streams and spitting pomegranate seeds at the gazelles that frisk beside them.

The shaven Buddhists with their silver begging bowls squat in orange robes, whirling brass prayer wheels beneath bell-tinkling pagoda towers and banyan trees, stirred by a private, tender-fingered wind. In the Shinto section there are vast inverted pyramids whose design would be envied by Frank Lloyd Wright, housing numberless family ancestors in airy apartments with sliding doors, rice-paper walls and rice-straw mats. They are fitted with enormous vats of hot water where families up to and including the eleventh generation bathe delightedly together in conversational hurly-burly.

In Heaven we find dour and skeptical Hebrew commentators with the harsh, hooked noses of their Hittite predecessors and fur-trimmed cartwheel hats; pagan roisterers from Euboea, Thessaly, Epirus and the Balearics, all joyfully cavorting; the Bindusaran king Asoka, parchment-faced Milarepa, Akhnaton, Baldur, Thor, Freya, Moloch (sour and ill-at-ease), Marduk, Ashur, Shiva, Teshub, Ishtar and Kybele, the lares and penates, Zeus, Bacchus, Hebe the cup-bearer, and, sitting side by side with suspicious and resentful looks, Martin Luther and the Pope whose episcopic agents fought him. And, in the Christian preserve, populated with its anchorites and eremites and hermits, dwell the diaphanous-gowned saints of Western imagery, propelled into the celestial ionosphere by man's frantic dream of escaping death.

Among this agreeable company we note Saint Eulalia, patroness of the Nepenthean sailors, of whom it is related: "She was born in 1712 at a remote village in the Spanish province of Estremadura. Various divine portents accompanied her birth. Her mother dreamed a strange dream about a sea-serpent; her father was cured of a painful gouty affection: the image of Saint James of Compostela in the local church was observed to smile benignly at the very hour of her entry into the world. At the age of two years and eleven months she took the vow of chastity. Much difficulty was experienced in keeping the infant alive; she tormented her body in so merciless a fashion. She refused to partake of food save once in every five weeks; she remained immovable 'like a statue' for months on end; she wore under her rough clothing iron spikes which were found, after death, to have entered deeply into her flesh. She was never known to use a drop of water for purposes of ablution or to change her underwear more than once a year, and then only at the order of her confessor who was obliged to be in daily contact with her. The heat of her body was such that it could not be touched by human hands. During her frequent trances she spoke accurately in sixty-nine different languages; there was no hair whatever on her head which was 'spotless as an egg.' She put baskets of sea urchins into her bed and, as a penance for what she called 'her many sins,' forced herself to catch the legions of vermin that infested her brown blanket, count them, separate the males from the females, set them free once more, and begin over again. She died at the age of fourteen years and two months. Her corpse forthwith became roseate in colour, exhaled a delicious odour of violets for twenty weeks, and performed countless miracles. On dissection, a portrait of Saint James of Compostela was discovered embedded in her liver."

We see the little-known Saint Oran, a friend and

follower of Saint Columba, who was buried at Icolm-
kill. His pretensions to sainthood are perhaps dubious.
It appears that he consented to be buried alive to
placate certain earth demons who were obstructing
the efforts of Columba to build a chapel. Columba
caused the body of his friend to be dug up after three
days. Oran, to the scandal of his colleagues, sat bolt
upright and announced there was no God, no judgment and no future after death. He had no time to
make further pronouncements. Columba pushed him
back into his coffin, slammed the lid and had him
buried deeper than before. The chapel, however,
which the demons were no longer able to topple,
and its cemetery were named Reilig Ouran. In mem-
ory of this saint's rigid celibacy, no women were allowed to pray or to be interred there.

Here are the beast-loving Irish saints: Bridget, who,
when cooking bacon for her father, bestowed a goodly
portion on a very hungry, miserable hound that
begged for it; Saint Patrick, who stopped some men
about to kill a fawn and carried it in his arms while
the doe ran behind; and Saint Columcille, who, as
he lay dying, was approached by his old white horse,
who shed tears in his lap. "Let him alone," murmured
Columcille to those who would have driven away
the animal, "for he loves me."

Among these blessed dead most certainly we have
the Greek Saint John of Cappadocia, whose liturgy
is authorized by Leontios the Nazeanzene. This
modest eligible among Heaven's Johns was born as

Ivan in Russia and taken prisoner by the Tartars, who sold him to an Ottoman Turkish officer in Prokopion, Cappadocia. There, despite threats and blandishments, he refused to embrace Islam. We are informed by the liturgy:

"One day the Mohammedan [officer] decided to go to Mecca. He stayed many months accompanied by many slaves and followers. While her husband was away the Hanum gave a large party for all her husband's relations, so that they might eat and pray for the master's safe return. John was serving at table, willing and humble as always. The pilaf was passed around. 'My husband's favorite dish; if only he were here to partake of it,' said the Hanum. 'It shall be done,' said the slave, 'just hand me his plate.' Everyone laughed sarcastically. 'The slave is hungry and wants some food,' they said. Then the slave went to his stable and prayed, 'Oh you who once in Babylon, answering the prayers of the prophet Abbakum, brought invisible food to Daniel in the lion's den, please answer my prayer too and send this food to my master in Mecca.'

"Some days later the master returned and asked who it was who had brought his own decorated copper plate to him in Mecca full of delicious pilaf still warm. And they answered, 'It was your slave.' And those who had laughed at him believed and honored him and his master set him free to go where he pleased. But John chose to remain in his dark stable, disdaining human vanities."

In 1730 this extraordinary saint died. Three years later his body was exhumed and found sweet and incorrupt. It was placed in a church that was burned in 1832 by Hadji Nedjeroglu Osman's soldiers, marching against the apostate king of Egypt. But John's remains survived untouched and were responsible for many miracles. Such a valuable trait was envied by the monks of the Russian monastery of Saint Pantelei-mon the Healer on Mount Athos. They negotiated with the people of Prokopion and purchased the saint's right hand. The rest of the body was smuggled to a village in Euboea, in 1924, after the Greco-Turkish war, when the Cappadocian Greeks had fled Asia Minor. John arrived in a caïque beneath a cargo of coal. He was installed in a silver-girt, glass-covered casket. His skin has become like boot leather and his features are no longer intact.

In Heaven we have Saint Nazarius, whose blood remained fresh and was manufactured into paste, some of which was sent to the Bishop of Brescia; the royal Saint Oswald, whose right arm never rotted, as Ingulphus testifies; Saint Hippolytus, who was rent by wild horses while he murmured: "Lord, they tear my body, receive Thou my soul," and the faithful followed behind sopping up his blood in sponges.

There are the Venerable Henry Heath, that indomitable Englishman who challenged his executioners: "Let them gnaw my flesh with their teeth"; the Blessed Andrew Bobola, slashed and flayed by the Cossack Assavould; and Athanasius, the Patriarch, called by Saint Gregory Nazeanzene "of an angelical disposition; mild in his reproofs, and instructive in his commendations."

Oh, let us call the heavenly roll. Saint John Before the Latin Gate who, when ordered cast into a pot of boiling oil, rejoiced aloud that he would soon join his Redeemer; but the oil cherished him like a pleasantly refreshing bath. Saint Stanislas Sezepanowski, hacked apart by Russian soldiers; the eagles defended the pieces until his Polish followers could reassemble him in Cracow's old cathedral. Saint Boniface, the jolly steward of fourth-century Rome, who debauched his mistress Aglaea, enjoyed the local wine, but later survived a caldron of hot pitch and had to be beheaded. His miracle-making corpse was sold for a hundred pieces of gold.

There is Saint John Nepomucen, spitted and broiled by Wenceslaus the Slothful; the great Saint Quirinus, who swam in the Sava River with a millstone round his neck, preaching as he trod the muddy waters; and Saint Boniface of Mainz, a Devonshire man martyred by the Teutonic tribes together with Deacon Strichald and Gunderhar the monk.

We find Saint Nicander and Saint Marcian, who requested "that life which is immortal, not the fleeting life of this world," and were obligingly beheaded by the agent of Diocletian. And there is, of course, Saint John the Baptist, wearing a soft camel's-hair garment bound with a leathern girdle, making a meal of honey and heavenly grasshoppers, his neck ringed by a cicatrice. Saint Irenaeus of Lyon, whose skull was kicked through the streets like a soccer ball by skeptical Calvinists thirteen centuries after he had been martyred. Saint Withburge, a virgin slaughtered together with Saint Sexburga. Saint Felicitas, mother of the Seven Brothers, to whom the perplexed Publius complained before ordering a family execution: "Unhappy woman, is it possible you should think death so desirable as not to permit even your children to live, but force me to destroy them by the most cruel torments?" Also the Carthaginian Saint Eugenius, his tongue removed by royal order, and Saint Symphorosa, another mother of seven, who was racked together with her family at Tivoli, near Rome.

I discern Saint Mamas, Saint Zephyrinus, who confessed a heretic whipped all night by an angel, and the royal Saint Louis of France. There is twitching Saint Vitus, whom the Dalmatian Slavs particularly revered for their old pagan deity, Vidda. And Saint Augustine (or Austin), a decided intellectual who had once thought that "without sensual pleasures life itself would seem to him no life but a pain." He dealt harshly with his former friends, the African Manichaeans, the Priscillianists, the Origenists, while tightening his personal code: "Drunkenness is far from me; Thou wilt grant in Thy mercy that it never approach me; but gluttony sometimes steals upon Thy servant." And now the learned old bishop is dipping his hands in bowls of whey while lecturing the five hundred bishops of the Donatist sect in a letter addressed to Hell.

52

I can see the younger Saint Simeon Stylites, accompanied by a leopard on a leash. Also Saints Marcellus and Valerian of Tournus, who were tortured with iron hooks; Saint Pambo of Nitria, completing the basket on which he was working when he died; Saint Cloud or Chlodoardus, of France's first princely family; Saint Gorgonius, who was grilled, salted and vinegared; Saint John the Dwarf, Anchorite of Scete; and Saint Januarius of Naples, whose blood, preserved in a churchly vial, still melts, bubbles up and, upon the least motion, flows.

There is the virginal Saint Thecla, protomartyr of her sex, who could when she desired preserve herself from flames; Saint Cyprian the Magician; Saint Dionysius the Areopagite, Bishop of Athens, whose head was stolen from Constantinople by the Crusaders in 1205 and now rests in Soissons, a valuable possession; Saint Osith, a princess slain by Hubba the Dane; the Isaurian Saint Tarachus, who was questioned by Numerican Maximus, together with Saints Probus and Andronicus. As the interrogation proceeded in Cilicia, the governor, Maximus, said:

"Strip him naked, gird him, and stretch him on the rack. . . . Lay salt upon his wounds, and rub his sides with broken tiles. . . . Put a heavy chain about his neck, and another upon his legs, and keep him in close prison. . . . Break his jaws with a stone, and bid him leave off his folly. . . . Bring in a pan of burning coals, and hold his hands in the fire till they are burnt. . . . Hang him by the feet, with his head over a great smoke. . . . Bring vinegar and salt, and force them up his nostrils. . . . Put mustard into the vinegar, and thrust it up his nose. . . . Heat bars of iron, and apply them to his feet. . . . Hoist him on the rack, and let him be scourged with thongs of raw leather till his shoulders are flayed. . . . Shave his head, and lay burning coals upon it. . . . Apply the red-hot spits once more to his arm-pits and sides."

This treatment excited only mild interest in Tarachus, who announced: "You have disfigured my face; but have added new beauty to my soul. I fear not any of your inventions, for I am clothed with the divine armor." His remarks prompted Maximus to order out lions and tigers; but the beasts were not hungry. So the governor at last summoned his confectors, or gladiators, to dispatch with their swords Tarachus and his friends. They did.

Nearby I can see Saint Hilarion, the abbot of whom it is said, "he sprang like a rose out of thorns," and who lived on the remarkable diet of fifteen figs a day, all taken after sundown; Saint Theodoret, who was burned like a candle by the uncle of Emperor Julian the Apostate; Saint Edmund, who inherited the throne of East Anglia from his uncle, King Offa, was crowned at Burum on the Stour and shot by the infidels under Hinguar "till his body was covered with arrows like a porcupine."

Heaven is tenanted by Saint James Intercisus of Beth-Lapeta, a Persian, who, when approached by executioners with scimitars, said: "Why stand ye idle looking on? Why begin ye not your work?" First his fingers, one by one, and then his toes were neatly chopped. He cheerfully observed: "Now the boughs are gone, cut down the trunk." His followers collected twenty-eight pieces of his body, which are today renowned, especially among the Copts of Egypt and Ethiopia.

There is Saint Stephen of Constantinople, whose brains and bowels were left on the ground; Saint Saturninus of Toulouse, dragged on a hillside by a wild bull; and, of course, the great Basque Jesuit, Saint Francis Xavier, whose "corpse was interred on Sunday, being laid after the Chinese fashion, in a large chest, which was filled up with unslaked lime, to the end that the flesh being consumed, the bones might be carried to Goa. On the 17th of February, in 1553, the grave was opened to see if the flesh was consumed; but the lime being taken off the face, it was found ruddy and fresh coloured like that of a man who is in sweet repose. The body was in like manner whole, and the natural moisture uncorrupted . . . and the holy corpse exhaled an odour so fragrant and delightful that the most exquisite perfume came nothing near it."

There is Saint Thrasilla, whose knees were hard as camel hide from continual prayer and who ordered those trying to comfort her death agonies: "Depart! Make room! Jesus is coming!" There is the martyred Thomas à Becket, murdered in Canterbury Cathedral, his brains drawn out with the point of a sword and scattered on the floor.

In this agreeable assemblage we discover the older

Saint Simeon Stylites, who spent the last twenty years of his life on a pillar forty cubits high, three feet wide at the top, and in a single day made 1,244 reverences of adoration despite an ulcer in his foot, swarming with live maggots. There is Saint Theodosius the Cenobiarch, who died by will power alone to dedicate a community burial place and who taught that "the continual remembrance of death is the foundation of religious perfection."

I see Saint Kentigern Munghu, Bishop of Glasghu, a Pict, and Saint Macarius the Elder, an Egyptian, who warned his brethren: "Let our eyes pour forth floods of tears before we go hence, lest we fall into that place where tears will only increase the flames in which we shall burn." And Saint Wulstan of Worcester, who, in his youth, perceiving himself touched by wanton love on seeing a woman dance, withdrew to a thicket and bewailed his fault; and Saint Sebastian, a Gaul, who was slain by archers in Mauretania; and the chaste Saint Agnes, who was placed in a brothel by a Roman governor but whose would-be ravishers fell blind.

Here is Saint Anastasius, carried into Persia by Chosroes and strangled; Saint Juventinus, scourged in Antioch; Saint Polycarp of Smyrna, who was to be burned but "the flames forming themselves into an arch, like the sails of a ship swelled with the wind, gently encircled the body of the martyr. . . ."

There is Saint John Chrysostom, who told the ladies of Constantinople to cease using silks, jewels and

cosmetics but who dressed himself in his best attire
to meet death in Cappadocia; and Saint Ignatius of
Antioch, who, when pushed into a Roman amphi-
theatre, shouted: "I am the wheat of the Lord: I must
be ground by the teeth of these beasts to be made the
pure bread of Christ." The church fathers comment:
"Two fierce lions being let out upon him, they instantly devoured him, leaving nothing of his body but
the larger bones; thus his prayer was heard."

Nearby reclines Saint Agatha, who, when her
breast was to be sliced off, reproached the executioner:
"Cruel tyrant, do you not blush to torture this part
of my body, you that sucked the breasts of a woman
yourself?" but was later rolled naked over live coals
mixed with potsherds. And Saint Romuald, of the
Ravenna ducal family of Honesti, who refused all
spices in his gruel, rebuking those who would feed
him better and saying: "Oh, gluttony, gluttony, thou
shalt never taste this: perpetual war is declared against
thee."

I see the unfortunate Saint Leander of Seville, who
suffered from gout (an affliction shared by the author
and by Saint Gregory, who died of it); Saint Abraham,
a Mesopotamian who married a noble woman but
never consummated the ceremony, advising his bride
that he preferred virginity to her; and Saint Julian of
Cilicia, who was drowned in a sack of scorpions and
vipers.

There is Saint Bennet or Benedict, whose monastery at Monte Cassino was blown up by Americans

and captured by exiled Poles; Saints Jonas and Bara-
chisius, who told King Sapor of Persia they refused
to worship the sun and moon, fire and water and
were sacrificed by freezing and by grilling *a la plancha*
on red hot plates; Saint Benjamin, impaled on a
knotty stake; the Blessed Herman Joseph of Cologne,
who went about ordering peasants to swat him in
the face "on account of my being a most filthy and
abominable creature, and because I cannot meet with
so much contempt as I deserve"; and Saint Mary of
Egypt, who ate only lentils, and who was buried by
Zosimus, aided by a lion.

There is Saint Teresa of Avila, who once was taken
to Hell. The entrance was a gloomy passage at the end
of which was a pool of putrid water alive with writhing snakes. She fancied she was thrust into a hole in
a wall where she could neither sit nor lie, and in that
position was tortured with cramps. Her life was a life
of suffering and, before she came to Heaven, she
advised her nuns: "You must pardon me much; you
must pardon me most of all the bad example I have
given you. Do not imitate me. Do not live as I have
lived. I have been the greatest sinner in all the world.
I have not kept the laws I made for others." And
Saint Chrysostom, who cautioned: "Depart from the
highway and transplant thyself in some inclosed
ground; for it is hard for a tree which stands by the
wayside, to keep her fruit, till it be ripe." And Saint
Thomas Aquinas. He proclaimed: "The soul is finite,
and God is infinite. The disproportion between the

two is so enormous (being, in fact, infinite in itself)
that the mere comparison must have a crushing effect
upon the finite being."

And the sweetest of them all, John of the Cross. He
knew the color of a soul's garment (white, green and
purple). He knew hope as a shield protecting the
soul from the arrows of the world. And in "the dark
night and dry purgation of desire," he wrote the finest
poetry in Heaven (save for David's): "Mios son los
cielos, y mia es la tierra, mias son las gentes, los justos
son mios, y mios los peccadores, los angelos son mios,
y la madre de dios y todas las cosas son mias, y el
mismo dios es mio y para mi, porque XPO es mio y
todo para mi; pues y pides y buscas alma mia tuyo
es todo esto y todo es para ti."

What are the qualities of all these lovely saints,
most of whom (like most gods) pertain to the Mediterranean world? Some are garbed in the down of
swans' breasts and some in sackcloth; some wear egret
feathers and some armor; some were sweet smelling,
even after death, and others as they burned turned
their bodies into purified gold, fragrant of spices.
Some are flame-proof like asbestos; some are indigesti-
ble to carnivores; some have decoagulating blood and
veins which clearly never suffered from cholesterol.
The fragments of their bones have great commercial
value.

All were truly noble, dedicated spirits, and all are
dead, their great common attribute. All discovered
that the world and the flesh could best be escaped

by running away, for, as Thomas Aquinas said: "It is a great thing, a very great thing, to be able to do without all solace, *both* human and divine, and to be able to bear this exile of the heart."

Together they inhabit the heaven of our imagination, a pleasant and fantastic place of sevenfold meaning, with its own secret mysteries and motions, direct and retrograde, of sextiles, quadrates, trines and oppositions, fiery trigons and aquatical trigons, shining in a night more lovely than the dawn, blessed by an eternity of existence we create for them, lying in the deep slumber of our dreams.

Ah! Could this but be. Heaven, the triumph over death, filled with a goodly, conscious company; the answer to the problem that gnaws within us as we live to die, languishing in expectancy and hope, and dying until our dying day.

FOUR

The Death of Kings

IT IS NOT necessary that a king should live well; indeed, the roster of those who have done so by any standard is surprisingly slim. But to die well is a royal requisite. People expect fine dying from their rulers.

This is part of the aristocratic heritage of monarchs. They have been bred by long blood lines to show us the path to eternity with courage and disdain. The plebeians of this unhappy world have little use for such sovereigns as Hadrian, Galba, Nero, Otho, Vitellius, Caracalla, Ivan the Terrible or the Scottish Kenneth, who, after lives of malicious evil, could not even properly face death.

There is something atavistic in mankind that seems to demand a violent end for kings. The Fire and Water kings of Cambodia were stabbed when they fell ill. The Congolese Chitomé believed the world would perish if their kings died naturally, so they strangled and clubbed them when they sickened. The priests of Meroë, in Ethiopia, sent word to their kings when the time had come to die. The tribes of African Fazoql hanged their rulers in knife-bladed nooses. The Sudanese Shilluk strangled their kings in specially-erected huts when they could no longer satisfy their wives. Matabele kings were speared when their hair turned gray. The kings of Dahomey were choked when presented with parrots' eggs by discontented ministers. The Samorins of medieval Calicut had their throats cut after twelve years' rule. In Bengal, whoever killed the king succeeded as king, until he too was slain. A similar custom prevailed in Passier, on Sumatra.

Throughout early Mediterranean history it was tribal custom to do away with sovereigns. From the isles of Spain to the isles of Greece the first deities were women, queen goddesses who took to themselves a series of sacred and temporary kings and then only for purposes of fertilization. At the end of each year the king was slaughtered in favor of a new husband chosen to replace him. This was a ritual and religious death. Sometimes the king was torn apart by savage women; sometimes he was stabbed with a sting ray's spear; sometimes he was axed, sometimes pierced with poison arrows, sometimes drowned, burned or hurled from a cliff.

After the Hellenic bands invaded Greece and joined

their male military aristocracy to the primitive female theocracy they found there, the king began to assume a greater role. He was gradually accepted as representative of Zeus, Poseidon, Apollo or other divinities. His reign was lengthened to eight years and was eventually terminated only by a proxy death for sacrificial purposes. Instead of the monarch, a boy was slain. Later still, animals were deemed sufficient. The Achaeans and the Dorians brought about kingships for a full natural life with patrilineal succession.

But the tradition of regicide remained embedded in man's mind. There is something particularly dreadful yet splendid about this political and semireligious kind of murder. This has made it fascinatingly attractive to societies both primitive and complex. When subjects kill their king they subconsciously feel they free themselves. And, deeper within their collective hidden minds, they kill their god.

Shaka, the dreadful nineteenth-century Zulu, called "the African Attila," was pierced with assegais by his two half-brothers, Mhlangana and Dingane. In tribal chants he was hailed as "Thou that art black, thou that art vast as the sea." Yet, when he saw death staring at him from their eyes, he wailed: "Ye children of my father, what is the wrong?" But the half-brothers made no answer. They advanced upon him. He turned to flee and tripped across the kraal-gate, where they caught him and stabbed him as he sought to scramble to his feet. All night his body lay there, while silence hung over the kraal. Next morning some menials rolled him up in a black oxhide and bundled him and his possessions into an empty corn pit. "There were no tears, only a numbness in the minds and hearts of his people."

However a king died, it was for long a custom in many parts of Africa that he should be accompanied to the world of shades by adequate numbers of wives, retainers and servants. We find this pitiless habit mirrored in the papyri of old Egypt and in Karnak's blazing Valley of the Kings. When I was in Togoland some years ago, the Awoamefia or paramount chief of Anlo, a sandspit on the Guinea Gulf, lay dying of age and cancer. This absolute ruler, Togbe Sri II, fond of champagne and whiskey and a member of Britain's Most Excellent Order of St. Michael and St. George, was entitled to take two hundred subjects with him when he expired, especially selected and slain for the signal honor. Akan and Ashanti police were moved in by the British to insure that the sovereign traveled alone.

Alexander of Macedon, a self-proclaimed divinity, was one of the ancient world's few monarchs who did not die of violence. A handsome, square-jawed man, according to the magnificent silver coin image of his countenance in Peshawar's modest museum, he was struck down by fever. But blood was usually the attribute of classical royal death. Priam, monarch of Troy, was dragged before the altar of its ruined capital and stabbed and decapitated by Pyrrhus. "Now his mighty trunk lies extended on the shore, the head torn from its shoulders, and a nameless corpse."

Crying, "Why this is violence," Caesar, who himself refused kingship but bequeathed his name to emperors, was stabbed by Casca. "When he saw that he was beset on every side by drawn daggers, he muffled his head in his robe, and at the same time drew down its lap to his feet with his left hand, in order to fall more decently, with the lower part of his body also covered. And in this wise he was stabbed with three and twenty wounds, uttering not a word, but merely a groan at the first stroke, though some have written that when Marcus Brutus rushed at him, he said in Greek, 'You too, my child.' "

The murder of Caligula was foretold by many extraordinary signs: a statue of Jupiter laughed so loud it frightened nearby workers; the capitol at Capua was struck by lightning; another bolt damaged the doorkeeper's room at the Roman palace. Sulla, a soothsayer, predicted the emperor's end. Caligula himself dreamt he was kicked by the gods. Blood spattered him when he made the propitiatory sacrifice of a flamingo. Then, when he was watching the rehearsal of some young Asian actors, he was slain by conspirators.

"Some say that . . . Chaerea came up behind and gave him a deep cut in the neck . . . and that then the Tribune Cornelius Sabinus . . . stabbed him in the breast. Others say that Sabinus, after getting rid of the crowd through Centurions who were in the plot, asked for the watchword, as soldiers do, and that when Gaius [Caligula] gave him 'Jupiter,' he cried 'So be it,' and as Gaius looked around, he split his jawbone with a blow of his sword. As he lay upon the ground and with writhing limbs cried out that he still lived the others dispatched him with thirty wounds, for the general signal was 'Strike again.' Some even thrust their swords through his privates. . . . With him died his wife Caesonia, stabbed with a sword by a Centurion, while his daughter's brains were dashed out against a wall." The gardens in which his corpse was interred were afterward disturbed by ghosts.

The deified Claudius was poisoned. Some said the poisoner was his taster, the eunuch Halotus. Others claimed that at a family dinner Agrippina, his wife, served the drug to him in mushrooms, a dish of which he was inordinately fond. Accounts also differ on what then occurred. Many say that as soon as he swallowed the poison he became speechless, and after suffering agony all night, died just before dawn. Others assert he fell into a stupor, threw up, and was given a second dose, perhaps in a gruel, under pretense that he must be refreshed. His death was kept quiet until arrangements had been completed on the succession. Accordingly vows were offered for his safety, as if he were still ill but alive. (This trick of pretending that a dead sovereign was still living has been played in other courts. The body of a Moroccan sultan renowned for his military talents was borne, propped up in a litter, through days of battle to hearten his troops.)

Vitellius, when surrounded by enemies, hid in a gatekeeper's lodge whose door he barricaded with a couch. When he was dragged from his hiding place, he pretended he was not the emperor. But he was recognized and arrested. "They bound his arms behind his back, put a noose about his neck, and dragged him with rent garments and half-naked to the Forum. All along the Sacred Way he was greeted with mockery and abuse, his head held back by the hair, as is common with criminals, and even the point of a sword placed under his chin, so that he could not look down but must let his face be seen. Some pelted him with dung and ordure, others called him incendiary and glutton, and some of the mob even taunted him with his bodily defects. He was in fact abnormally tall, with a face usually flushed from hard drinking, a huge belly, and one thigh crippled from being struck once upon a time by a four-horse chariot. . . . At last on the Stairs of Wailing he was tortured for a long time and then dispatched and dragged off with a hook to the Tiber."

Domitian expired bravely. He was first stabbed in the groin and then slain, with seven wounds, by Clodianus, a subaltern; Maximus, a freed slave; Satur, his head chamberlain, and a gladiator. The emperor grappled with one of the assassins, "trying now to wrest the dagger from his assailant's hands and now to gouge out his eyes with his lacerated fingers."

Certain kings, like England's Harold, died fighting for their people. John of Bohemia, a valiant old warrior, insisted on a battlefield death despite his blindness. Said he to his knights: "Gentlemen, you are all my men, my friends, my companions. I beg you to lead me forward that I may strike a blow this day." The knights led him forward, fastening the reins of their horses together, putting their king in front to gratify his wish. He rode in among the enemy, hacking with his sword. The next day the king was found among his dead knights with their horses all tied together.

Beowulf, ruler of the Geats, was killed in combat with a fire-breathing dragon. "The bold king again had mind of his glory; with might his glaive was driven into the dragon's head,—blow nerved by hate. But Naegling was shivered, broken in battle was Beowulf's sword, old and gray. Twas granted him not that ever the edge of iron at all could help him at strife: too strong was his hand, so the tale is told, and he tried too far with strength of stroke all swords he wielded, though sturdy their steel: they steaded him nought. Then for the third time thought on its feud that folk-destroyer, fire-dread dragon, and rushed on the hero, where room allowed, battle-grim, burning; its bitter teeth closed on his neck, and covered him with waves of blood from his breast that welled."

Not all soldier-princes ended so vividly. Other conquerors than Alexander succumbed in bed. Noble Saladin, a Syrian Kurd who made life so miserable for the Crusaders, caught fever in a heavy rainstorm. "Each day the Sultan grew worse, his head was racked with pain, and he suffered internally. On the fourth day the doctors bled him; and from that time he grew steadily worse. The fever parched his skin, and he became weaker and weaker. On the ninth day his mind wandered; he fell into a stupor. . . . On Sunday, the tenth day of the illness, medicine gave some relief. . . . On Tuesday night there was a divine with him, repeating the confession of faith and reading the Holy Word; and when he came to the passage 'He is God, than whom there is no other God,—who knoweth the unseen and the seen,—the Compassionate, the Merciful,' the Sultan murmured, 'True'; and when the words came, 'In Him do I trust,' the dying man smiled, his face lighted up, and he rendered his soul to his Lord."

Genghis Khan, who boasted he was God's scourge, fell ill far from his Mongolian homeland "on the 15th day of the middle autumn month of the Year of the Swine" (August 18, 1227). As he lay stricken, he gave orders that his forthcoming death be kept secret until the succession over his hordes was arranged and that his body be brought eastward for burial. He was assured by his respectful courtiers:

"O thou Lion of Mankind, wonderfully procreated by Eternal Heaven! O thou Teb-Tengri, my Sutu-Bogdo Khan of Khans! . . . Even though we could not shield thy splendid life against the onslaught of death, we should still carry thy remains, which are as precious as the finest jade, to thy home, that thy consort Bortei may look upon them, as would be the wish of the whole of thy great people." They then bore him back to his homeland and buried him beneath a tree on a mountain where he used to rest after the hunt. The funeral cart was placed beside him, eight white tents were pitched as shrines and a thousand horsemen were stationed below the summit as a guard of honor.

Tamerlane, another great Tartar-Mongol khan, who made of Samarkand one of the world's finest cities and filled the Middle East with pyramids of human skulls, prepared with similar care for his death. Tamerlane respected gallant dying. He once pardoned a jester for joking in death's presence. When his own time came, he lay suffering with fever one February night in 1405. A storm raged outside. Flashes of lightning lit up his sickroom, where imams and sayids were reading the prescribed Koranic prayers.

His physicians told him there was no hope of survival and he sent for his wives and his emirs, telling them: "Do not make a lament or raise a clamor about my death, for such things do no good; never yet has death been frightened away by screaming. Instead of rending your garments and running hither and thither like lunatics, pray God to be gracious to me; say prayers that will delight my soul." Then he appointed Pir-Muhammed, his grandson, as successor, made the emirs swear to obey Pir-Muhammed and serve him faithfully. The emirs wanted to send for his

other grandsons, who were in command of sections
of the army, but Tamerlane knew it was too late. "I
have only one desire left, to see my son Shah Rokh
again," he said, "but that is impossible, Allah has
not willed it, so I must wait for the day of the Last
Judgment before my wish can be fulfilled."

Asoka-Vardhano, the famous North Indian ruler
who repented of his conquests and became a Buddhist
saint, died a sweet ascetic death of contemplation.
The philosopher kings of early Chinese dynasties died
in benevolent repose, as, indeed, has been the good
fortune of recent Scandinavian monarchs and, for
three centuries, those of England. Only one British
sovereign, Arthur, laid any claim to immortality. At
least, Sir Thomas Malory tells us that, at his last
moment:

"He was led away in a ship wherein were three
queens; that one was King Arthur's sister, Queen
Morgan le Fay; the other was the Queen of North-
galis; the third was the Queen of the Waste Lands.
Also there was Nimue, the chief lady of the lake, that
had done much for King Arthur. More of the death
of King Arthur could I never find, but that ladies
brought him to his burials; and such one was buried
there, that the hermit bare witness that sometime
was Bishop of Canterbury, but yet the hermit knew
not in certain that he was verily the body of King
Arthur: for this tale Sir Bedivere, knight of the Table
Round, made it to be written. Yet some men say in
many parts of England that King Arthur is not dead,

but had by the will of our Lord Jesu into another place; and men say that he shall come again, and he shall win the holy cross. I will not say it shall be so, but rather I will say: here in this world he changed his life."

Montezuma, ruler of the Aztecs, died a prisoner of Cortés, besieged with the Spaniards in the citadel of Mexico by obsidian-sworded, javelin-bearing soldiers of the war god Huichilobos (Huitzilopochtli). Wounded by stone missiles aimed at his Spanish captors, Montezuma fell senseless. He was borne to his apartments in Cortés's stronghold and, when he recovered consciousness, sat brooding upon his fate. He sickened rapidly, more from sadness at his captivity and the rising hatred for him of his own subjects than because of wounds. Father Olmedo, Cortés's confessor, sought to persuade him to accept Christianity and a deathbed baptism. Montezuma refused.

"When father Olmedo, therefore, kneeling at his side, with the uplifted crucifix, affectionately besought him to embrace the sign of man's redemption, he coldly repulsed the priest, exclaiming, 'I have but a few moments to live, and will not at this hour desert the faith of my fathers.' One thing, however, seemed to press heavily on Montezuma's mind. This was the fate of his children, especially of three daughters. . . . Calling Cortés to his bedside, he earnestly commended these children to his care, as 'the most precious jewels that he could leave him.' He besought the general to interest his master, the em-

74

peror, in their behalf, and to see that they should not be left destitute, but be allowed some portion of their rightful inheritance. 'Your lord will do this,' he concluded, 'if it were only for the friendly offices I have rendered the Spaniards, and for the love I have shown them,—though it has brought me to this condition! But for this I bear them no ill-will.' Such, according to Cortés himself, were the words of the dying monarch. Not long after, on the 30th of June, 1520, he expired in the arms of some of his own nobles, who still remained faithful in their attendance on his person. 'Thus,' exclaims a native historian, one of his enemies, a Tlascalan, 'thus died the unfortunate Montezuma, who had swayed the sceptre with such consummate policy and wisdom; and who was held in greater reverence and awe than any other prince of his lineage, or any, indeed, that ever sat on a throne in this Western World. With him may be said to have terminated the royal line of the Aztecs.' "

The Russian tsars, whose line finally terminated before a Bolshevik firing squad in an Ekaterinburg cellar, lived in constant dread of death, the unfortunate Nicholases and Alexanders. Their heritage was desolate and bloody. Ivan the Terrible slew his son in a fit of rage; later he developed a psychopathic terror of his own end and could not be comforted by soothsayers and astrologers. He went "in fear of an appointed hour that had been foretold to him by somebody or other, and could find no peace. He tormented

himself beyond measure and hardly knew which way
to turn; he mortified the flesh, prayed, wept, shrieked,
cursed, and frittered away his remaining strength in
senseless fear of death and of the Last Judgment.
Again and again he called for a refutation of the
prophecy and did not want to die. Then, again, he
would think he felt better and make fun of those who
interpreted the heavens. His last day was drawing
near. Ivan had had the gems from his treasure chamber displayed before him again and questioned his
foreign confidants about their healing properties and
deeper symbolic meaning. He then sat down to play
chess. But while he was moving the pieces, he fell
back and died."

Kings who are slain in hot blood, like so many
Roman emperors, often died abjectly and in craven
terror. My friend Radoje Janković, who helped to
murder the last Obrenović ruler of Serbia and his
wife, told me that Miloš ended his days contempti-
bly. Conspiratorial officers burst into the Belgrade
palace, where they found the queen and hacked her
to pieces. But they searched unsuccessfully for their
sovereign until they discovered him cowering in a
closet, dressed in a silk nightgown. They dragged him
out screaming, stabbed him and hurled him through
a window. His hands caught the sill and he clung
there, in a desperate effort to survive. Janković, who
later became a diplomat under another dynasty,
sliced off the royal fingers with his saber and they

wiggled in reflex as the body dropped on a manure heap in the garden.

How implacably and even with what triteness death reaches for its most pretentious victims. At Berkeley, wicked Isabella and Mortimer sought to extinguish the immured Edward II after Bishop Orleton had preached a seditious sermon, using the text "My head, my head" to demonstrate that the sick head of the state could not be restored by all the remedies of Hippocrates and would therefore have to be cut off. When Edward refused to die, they had him barbarously murdered. Then, as befitted a crowned king of England, he was buried in the Benedictine Abbey Church of St. Peter, Gloucester.

In more recent centuries formal regicide has usually been the procedure, carried out with cold, courageous dignity, giving the masses a chance to share in this atavistic crime. Queen Mary of Scotland, King Charles of England and France's Marie Antoinette died regally and well. Mary had a splendid sense of drama. She dressed with precise perfection for her execution, wearing a black velvet robe of state, stamped with gold, and a black stomacher. Her master of household carried the long train of her dress. Attached to her wig was a stiff white veil and upon her feet were shoes of soft Spanish leather. She bore a linen handkerchief with golden fringe so that her eyes might be properly bound. And her underclothes were crimson so that they should not be crudely marred by spurting blood.

When Melville, her master of household, was instructed by Elizabeth's court to inform the royal prisoner her hour had come, Mary said: "Today, good Melville, thou seest the end of Mary Stuart's miseries, and that should rejoice thee. I pray thee carry a message from me that I die a true woman of my religion, like a true Queen of Scotland and France. But God forgive them that have long desired my end and thirsted for my blood, as the hart does for the water-brooks. Commend me to my dearest and most sweet son [the future King James I]. Tell him I have done nothing to prejudice him in his realm, nor to disparage his dignity."

A special scaffold had been erected in a royal hall, equipped with black-hung rails, a black stool, black cushion and black chopping block. Beside it were seats for Queen Elizabeth's representatives, the Earls of Shrewsbury and Kent. At the rear stood two masked executioners in black, wearing white aprons. And, guarded by soldiers, two hundred noble witnesses waited below.

Kent, a grim Protestant, would not permit final popish trumperies" for the Catholic victim, but she kissed a crucifix and said: "Even as Thy arms, O Jesu Christ, were spread here upon the cross, receive me into the arms of mercy, and forgive me all my sins. Amen." Then Bulle, the executioner, and his assistant kneeled before Mary to beg her forgiveness. She replied: "I forgive you with all my heart. For I hope this death shall give an end to my troubles."

Mary was then partially disrobed by her ladies-in-waiting, Jane Kennedy and Elizabeth Curle. Dressed only in her crimson undergarments, she embraced the two weeping women and said: "Ne cry vous, j'ay preye pur vous." She knelt on the cushion afterwards and intoned the psalm: "In te, domine, confido, me confundar in aeternum." Then Bulle raised his axe.

"The first blow fell awry, striking the back of the head instead of severing the neck. A hollow groan escaped from the mouth of the victim. At the second stroke, the axe sank deep into the neck, and the blood spurted out copiously. Not until a third blow had been given was the head detached from the trunk. Now came a further touch of horror. When Bulle wished to lift the head by the hair and show it to those assembled, he gripped only the wig, and the head dropped on to the ground. It rolled like a ball across the scaffold; and when the executioner stooped once more to seize it, the onlookers could discern that it was that of an old woman with close-cropped and grizzled hair. For a moment, the spectators were overcome by their feelings, so that all held their breath in silence. At length, however, when the executioner lifted up the head and shouted: 'God save the queen!' the Dean of Peterborough summoned up courage to say: 'Amen! Amen! So perish all the queen's enemies.' The Earl of Kent came up to the dead body and, with lowered voice, said: "Such end happen to all the queen's and Gospel's enemies!' Unnoticed, Mary's Skye terrier had crept beneath her petticoat. Now the little beast sprang forth 'embrued in her blood.' Afterwards, 'it would not depart from the dead corpse, but came and lay between her head and shoulders.' "

Mary's grandson, Charles Stuart, displayed equal dignity when Cromwell had him killed. He instructed the executioner to set the block firmly and "have a care of the axe." He regarded with contempt some ingenious ropes and pulleys designed to drag him down if he should prove unwilling to submit. He then discarded his cloak and put on a white cap, under which his long curls were tucked to keep his neck bare, advising the bishop who would comfort him: "I am going from a corruptible to an incorruptible crown, where no disturbance can be." The executioner then, as was traditional, fell on his knees and asked for pardon.

" 'The King cannot pardon a subject who willfully sheds his blood,' Charles answered: then added quickly, implicitly restoring the humanity of the situation: 'I pray you, do not put me to pain.' The King moved to the edge of the scaffold and for a moment it seemed that he was, after all, to make an attempt to speak to the tight-wedged, silent crowd. But he only looked—as those in the street noticed—toward St. James and smiled. Then he spoke again to the executioner: 'I shall say but a short prayer and, when I hold out my hands thus, strike.' For a minute or two he stood in profound meditation. Then he murmured to himself a few notable words before he lay down with his head over the block and could no longer be seen by the spectators in the street. They saw nothing but the flash of the upraised axe before it crashed down and killed the King at its first falling. Young Philip Henry in the crowd left it on record: 'At the instant when the blow was given there was such a dismal universal groan amongst the thousands of people who were in sight of it as it were with one consent, as I never heard before and desire I may never hear again.' "

Beautiful young Marie Antoinette, the Austrian queen of France, rode to her death in a tumbril amid the jeers of a hostile crowd; but she carried it off with grace. The officer in charge of conveying her cart to the guillotine forced his horse through the multitude yelling: "Here she is, the wicked Antoinette. She is done for, my friends." Cannon fired salvos from the Invalides and the Bastille and the brutal *tricoteuses*, wearing red bonnets and carrying pikes, screamed for blood.

Paris's Place de la Révolution, now Place de la Concorde, was black with people as the cart bearing the proudly impassive queen rattled in. When the guillotine itself was reached, Marie Antoinette climbed the ladder without accepting help, losing one of her little purple shoes. On the platform, by mistake, she trod on the executioner's foot. "Monsieur," she said, "I ask your pardon. I did not do it on purpose." Those were her last words. She shut her eyes. She was dragged to a long plank that was tipped over and a heavy wooden collar was fastened about her neck.

Then the blade hurtled down.

One of the assistants picked up her dripping head by the powdered hair, and, to applause, carried it round the scaffold. A man emerged from beneath the scaffold, his shoes covered with blood, holding a blood-stained handkerchief in his hand and a carnation between his teeth. He was arrested. Then a cart, streaming blood, rattled toward the Madeleine cemetery. There the executioners noticed that no grave had been prepared. Anxious to get their dinners, they threw the body on the grass.

One by one death claimed these proud rulers: mad emperors fleeing their legionaries' knives down the labyrinthine corridors of Roman palaces; clubbed and strangled Congolese; warrior princes of the Geats, Bohemians and Saxons; marvelous Tartar-Mongol khans and Arab sultans; Aztec kings and Russian tsars; Scottish, French and English sovereigns. Some of them welcomed death and some fought it; some masked their thoughts in pride. The terrible Ivan feared it and Miloš clung yammering to its ledge. But, as cruel, wise Tamerlane remarked before eternity engulfed him: "Never yet has death been frightened away by screaming." Death embraces kings with the same indifference as commoners.

FIVE

Death in the Name of God

"*He wahine, he whenua i mate ai te tangata,*" said the Maoris of New Zealand, "Women and land are the reasons why men die." This is, of course, not true. Men die because they cannot escape death. And, knowing this, in their own image they have invented gods; in their own pitiful craving they have imagined resurrection and eternity, conscious eternity, an eternity in which they can partake. Poor man: since first he gave being to the sun and stars he has sought to mesmerize himself into acceptance of these sweet beliefs.

Without death there would not be religion, for divinity imposes itself on man by fear. Love comes later. And the only creed that truly teaches love is Buddhism, a creed which formally disbelieves in God.

Man is prepared to accept life but not death. Therefore he lets death's inexplicable presence persuade him there must be a pattern to existence. "Physical Teleology impels us," says Kant, "it is true, to seek a Theology: but it cannot produce one."

This desperate search to build a rational fantasy permitting us to flee death has led man to his most evil sin: killing in death's (or God's) own name. For, even were He to exist, only God Himself should be allowed to kill for God. Yet man insists on imitating the image he has alone projected, an image which, he claims, distinguishes him from beast. He invented the word "God," he interprets the word "God"; and he appropriates to himself the right to slaughter in the name of God.

This is a wicked justification of death and faith in death. And religions, which all too often curse man for taking his own life, the only fate he can justifiably control, will bless him all too often for stealing the life of a fellow human being.

Religious killing shows man at his most depraved; for in this act he destroys the beauty of his dream by pretending to divine power. From this savagery, excused in the name of the Lord, we see the development of fanaticism.

Regard Hasan ibn-al-Sabbah, the withered Old Man of the Mountain. In 1090 he founded the dervish order of Assassins (or hashish eaters) whose holy dope addicts sneaked from their Persian hidey-hole of Alamut to kill for Allah's sake. Disguised as merchants, as pilgrims, as beggars, they wandered through the countryside and slaughtered by dagger, believing such ecstasy would insure them paradise. Regard Conchubar, the bloodthirsty Welsh Christian king who, when he could find no Jews to slay, rushed out with his sword and hacked the branches of an oak tree until he fell lifeless in his passion.

Simpler creeds, perplexed by pagan doubt, sought only to kill death itself, not man. The old Franks made a straw image of death which they carried away from their villages, flinging it into a swift-flowing stream. Similar effigies were fashioned by the early Teutons of Silesia, torn to shreds and buried under oaks. The Balinese tried to rob death of its terror by living in great families with the spirits of their ancestors, happily cremating those who died but not seeking to precipitate their deaths.

Many amiable tribes attempted at least indirect resurrection without recourse to murder. Heitsi-eibib, god-hero of the Hottentots, had the unusual attribute of successively dying and returning to live again among his friendly children. The old Basque hunters thought they could perpetuate consciousness by exchanging souls with the bears and wolves they speared. The Aztecs developed a sacrament of communion in which they devoured the body of their Huitzlipochtli (Cortés' "Witchywolf") as crumbled dough. Such transubstantiation was familiar to the Indian Brahmins in the form of rice cakes long before Christianity developed a similar rite.

But human sacrifice, from earliest days until our own, has been considered a propitiation of those gods to whom man egocentrically ascribes a thirst for blood. The ancient Cypriots worshiped the ram-clutching, broad-nosed, spade-bearded, horned god Beš, from whose stone belly poured the sacrificial flood produced by the victims of stabbing priests. The Dravidian Khonds of Bengal cultivated turmeric, which, they held, could never attain proper hue without the shedding of blood.

The Leucadians fastened feathers and live birds to victims and hurled them into the sea from cliffs. The Toltecs cut the hearts from screaming youths to the contrapuntal sound of flutes. The Indians of Ecuador slew a hundred children annually to improve harvest prospects. The Pawnees of North America carved human offerings at spring sowing time; the Sioux painted girls red and black before roasting them. Guinea Negroes impaled maidens at the moment of vernal equinox and the Bechuana Marimos killed fat men at the time of seeding, first having the courtesy to make them drunk. The Lhota Naga of the upper Brahmaputra flayed boys alive and distributed pieces to farmers for insertion in corn bins. In Borneo it was considered obvious that before the gods would assure food to man a woman had to die.

From these convictions that murder could help man feed himself (in some cases, the corpse provided food; always it reduced the number of hungry mouths), man elaborated his creeds. He mixed them

88

with politics and intolerance as an excuse to satiate his need to slay in the names of invented gods. These maturing dogmas have marked, at one or another time, all faiths we boastfully call modern.

Abraham of the Jews, who slew Samaritans and Philistines, was ready to ungorge his son but had the ingenuity to substitute a ram. The early Christians suffered from the Romans. After they took power through Emperor Constantine, they applied well-learned techniques to other, less-enlightened people. The Moslems used the sword on those who would not accept Islam and thus, by no means incidentally, spread their temporal rule.

Blood and intolerance are symbols of religion and red is the color of all three: red, the hue of a rage to live and not the eternal black or white of death. This is the red of cardinals' birettas, of flaming autos-da-fé; the red that stains the golden robes of Buddhist priests deep orange; the red of Pravoslav chasubles, of Jewish sacrificial wine, of the Communion elixir in sects of Christ; the red in the Makhmal, borne to Mecca; the red that streams down chain-beat backs of Shiah mobs, the red of the belly-cut Shinto supplicant, the red of all those who would avoid death by conferring it.

I have seen the barren cemetery outside Mecca housing the bones of those who died so violently in search of the Prophet's horse-borne eternal life. In the ruined chapel of Nicaea on Turkish Iznik's shores, with crows cawing above, lie sepulchers of skulls and tibia that belonged to Arian priests. These were slaughtered at a religious conclave by their Athanasian colleagues for disagreeing on the meaning of the Christian sacraments. The more complex our tenets, the more dangerous they are.

Martin Luther, a sensible prelate in whose name, a century later, half of Europe was ravaged, said: "If I die in my bed, it will be a grievous shame to the Pope." Luther risked death often with rare devotion but cheated the torturers of Roman orthodoxy. Sixteenth-century medicine did for him instead.

Hus, Bruno and the other great reformers had less gentle handling from religion. Hus was unfrocked at Constance by his fellow priests and consumed by fire while he chanted hymns. Bruno was tortured so he should abjure his errors in interpreting the ways of God. Having done so, he was placed in the hands of the governor of Rome, who kindly recommended he be punished "with as great clemency as possible and without affection of blood" (the formula for burning at the stake). Bruno told his judges: "Greater perhaps is your fear in pronouncing my sentence than mine in hearing it." On the pyre he angrily turned his eyes from the crucifix, that symbol of eternal cruelty, and (says his contemporary, Kasper Schoppe) "he was burned and perished miserably, and is gone to tell, I suppose, in those other worlds of his fancy, how [the] blasphemous and impious are dealt with by the Romans."

John Foxe in his *Book of Martyrs* prepared a melancholy ledger of Christians killed in the name of various merciful gods, generally their own. The Romans, who saw in Christianity a politically subversive force (because it denied imperial divinity), rounded up its practicants and sewed them in the skins of beasts, worried them by dogs, dressed them in wax-stiffened shirts and set them aflame, racked them, broiled them, scourged them, stoned them, lacerated them with red-hot pincers or threw them on the horns of bulls. "Every wound is a mouth," said one of these unfortunates, the Palestinian Romanus, "to sing the praises of the Lord."

The Arian bishops of Alexandria, with the blessing of Byzance, persecuted the Athanasians in revenge for Nicaea, and "If a man accused of being an orthodox Christian made his escape, his whole family were massacred and his effects forfeited." When Julian the apostate emperor reverted to paganism, he turned a sardonic eye on all the squabbling Christians, thrust them into filthy sewers, goaded them with pointed sticks, smeared them with honey and left them to hungry wasps, all for the sake of more conservative and less pretentious gods.

The bishops of Carthage, followers of Arius, roasted their Athanasian opponents, among them Rusticus, Severus, Liberatus, Rogatus, Servus, Septimus and Boniface. Later Romish episcopates of Lyon and Toulouse sought out Henrician and Waldensian Christian deviationists and slew them, even though Peter Waldo, the anti-Papist, argued "he could not be silent in a cause of such importance as the salvation of men's souls, wherein he must obey God rather than man."

When the reformist Albigensians of Béziers insisted on doctrinal modifications, they were warned by a papal legate that "If all the city did not acknowledge their fault, they should taste of one curse without distinction of religion, sex or age." He shouted to his true-believing troops: "Kill them, kill them all; kill man, woman and child; kill Roman Catholics as well as Albigenses, for when they are dead the Lord knows how to select his own." And bold Simon de Montfort, pursuing the same heretics, took their castle of Beron and blinded the garrison, all but one man left with a single eye in order to lead them home (the same treatment, incidentally, applied by Emperor Basil of Byzantium to the army of Bulgaria's tsar).

Rev. Dr. Geddes tells us how the Spanish Inquisition arranged an auto-da-fé in the name of religious mercy. "The stakes of the protestants, or as the inquisitors call them, the professed, are about four yards high, and each have a small board, whereon the prisoner is seated within half a yard of the top. The professed then go up a ladder betwixt two priests, who attend the whole day of execution. When they come even with the board they turn about to the people, and the priests spend a quarter of an hour in exhorting them to be reconciled to the see of Rome. On their refusing, the priests come down, and the executioner ascending, turns the professed from off the ladder upon the seat, chains their bodies close to the stakes, and leaves them. . . . A general shout is then raised, and when the priests get off the ladder, the universal cry is, 'Let the dogs' beards be burnt,' which accordingly is done by means of flaming furzes thrust against their faces. This barbarity is repeated till their faces are burnt, and is accompanied with loud acclamations. Fire is then set to the furzes, and the criminals are consumed."

During the Counter-Reformation, Protestant Bohemians were smoked like hams by their Catholic cousins. They were hacked into small pieces. Their mouths were crammed with gunpowder and exploded. They were scourged with wires. They were placed upon the rack and mangled. Their feet were immersed in boiling lead. That noble clergyman, Jerome of Prague, wore to his execution a paper cap painted with red devils, of which he observed: "Our Lord Jesus Christ, when he suffered death for me a most miserable sinner, did wear a crown of thorns upon his head; and I, for his sake, will wear this adorning of derision and blasphemy."

Protestants and Catholics were infected with the same murderous virus during those curious violent sixteenth and seventeenth centuries that produced Shakespeare, the Pléiade, Michelangelo, Rembrandt, the loveliness of Baroque and the hideousness of religious war and torture. In England the hardy and romantic Elizabethans for the most part accepted without demur the usual sentence for those who were discovered to be priests ordained by the see of Rome in contempt of the English queen's crown and dignity. This was: "That you be drawn on a hurdle to the place of execution, and there be hanged by the neck; then whilst still alive be laid upon the ground, have your members amputated, your entrails drawn out of the body, you being still alive, and burned, your head cut off, and your body divided into four parts, and your head and quarters placed where the Lady the Queen has been pleased to appoint."

Mary, the unhappy wife of Spanish Philip, had of course defended the papal cause with equal vigor, leaving a legacy of savage bigotry and hatred. This had produced the sad and noble death of Latimer who, when they brought lighted faggots to his pyre, turned to his companion and pronounced these famous words: "Be of good comfort, Master Ridley, and play the man. We shall this day light such a candle, by God's grace, in England, as I trust shall never be put out." But Ridley, pitifully heaped with green shrubbery, called in woe: "Let the fire come unto me, I cannot burn."

Thousands of Christians who disagreed on sacramental questions murdered each other throughout the period we call the Renaissance because of its splendid cultural revival. Catherine de Médicis had French Huguenots massacred on St. Bartholomew's Day of 1572. In Münster, members of the local ministry were taken during the religious wars, stripped, blinded and pricked to death with darts. In Ireland dozens of so-called heretics were dragged by horses into bogs. And, when Napoleon's army took Madrid, they entered the chambers of the Inquisition and found:

"Instruments of torture of every kind which the ingenuity of men or devils could invent. The first instrument was a machine by which the victim was confined, and then, beginning with the fingers, all the joints in the hands, arms, and body were broken and drawn one after another, until the sufferer died. The second was a box in which the head and neck of the victim were so closely confined by a screw, that he could not move any way. Over the box was a vessel, from which one drop of water fell upon the head of the victim every second, each successive drop falling upon precisely the same place; by which, in a few moments, the circulation was suspended, and the sufferer had to endure the most excruciating agony. The third was an infernal machine, laid horizontally, to which the victim was bound; the machine then being placed between two beams, in which were scores of knives so fixed that, by turning the machine with a crank, the flesh of the sufferer was all torn from his limbs into small pieces."

Millions of men and women have indeed been helped by faith in divinity and superior forces to meet even the most unpleasant end, and courage is often the symbol of a True Believer. Unfortunately, however, all too often one brave sectarian has been cut

down by another brave sectarian and, throughout
history, organized religion has served as a tool for
politics. Under the Cross of the Crusaders, under the
six-point Star of David, under the Crescent of Islam
and even under Buddha's peaceful prayer wheel,
Bedouin, Samaritan, Philistine, Roman, Vandal,
Goth, Spaniard, Tamil and Khmer have killed and
been killed. Beš, Baal, Moloch and Huitzlipochtli;
Zeus, Thor and Yahweh; Wotan, Osiris, Mazda, Shiva,
Geb; Horus the falcon-faced, foam-formed Aphrodite;
the Lord of Arius, the Lord of Athanasius; ah, how
cruelly advocated are these gods. Maybe the furtive
Yezidi, still crouched in their Syrian villages, have the
most sensible solution. They see two forces contesting
for control, the good of God and the evil of the
Devil. Since God is said to be so good, they reason, he
will be benevolent if he triumphs; therefore let us
hedge our mortal bet by worshiping the Devil.

Powerful Arian prelates slew powerful Athanasians
and vice versa in an earthly power struggle. Similar
struggles encompassed Spanish Catholics, English
Protestants, Turkish Moslems, Khazar Jews and Cam-
bodian Hindus. Judas Iscariot sold the revolutionary
Jesus to the counter-revolutionary Romans, intent on
consolidating imperial orders and later Judas burst
asunder on the field of Aceldama, field of blood. Joan
of Arc was condemned for the sin of political opposi-
tion to the English crown, inquiring of Peter Mauricius,
magistrate of the bishops who judged her: "Magistrate
Peter, where will I pass from here today?" Thomas

à Becket, for opposing King Henry's material wishes, was cut down in his cathedral.

One would like to believe, in our smug times, that religion no longer is mixed with politics and the days are long since past when men must die because they worship in a particular way. Alas, such is not the case. The twentieth century can boast the most efficient, coldly calculated and cruel sectarian slaughters.

Even Hitler at first claimed the mantle of religion to excuse his persecutions. He told the Munich Burghers in 1922: "My feeling as a Christian points me to my Lord and Savior as a fighter. It points me to the man who once in loneliness, surrounded by a few followers, recognized these Jews for what they were and summoned men to fight against them. . . . How terrific was His fight for the world against the Jewish poison."

We know how he carried out his promises. The roster of Dachau tells us how "these Jews" died for being Jews. "Let the dog expire; that's what he's here for, see," said the SS guards. ". . . I saw the horribly contorted body of a prisoner lying at the foot of the electrified barbed wire fence." . . . "If the warder whistled the dog would bury his fangs in the genitals of the prisoner." " 'You ghetto swine.' Another terrible blow and the prisoner went down like a log."

At Belsen, Buchenwald, Auschwitz, Majdanek, Ravensbrück, Treblinka and other diabolical concentration camps the Jews were assembled, beaten and burned, for the sin of their religion. Professor Clauberg, an SS brigadier-general, was instructed by Heinrich Himmler to go to Ravensbrück and ascertain "the approximate time that would be required to sterilize one thousand Jewesses." Those women who did not die of the experiment were subsequently gassed. In Buchenwald "let me merely mention that sixty-eight Jews went mad that very first night. They were clubbed to death like mad dogs by Sommer, four men at a time." After the Germans took Riga, "occasionally starving Jews tried to trade a garment for a sandwich. Ghetto inmates caught in such an attempt first received twenty-five lashes and then were hanged."

While murdering Jews was officially encouraged in Germany, Russia, Poland, Slovakia and Rumania (where some were gutted and hung by the heels in butcher shops), as well as in the more frenzied Arab lands, this virus of sectarian killing spread elsewhere to other faiths. Buddhist Singhalese slaughtered Hindu Tamils in Ceylon. Sikh mobs in the Punjab battered Moslems to death and Moslems speared Sikhs, men, women and children, and cut their corpses to bits. India was partitioned on the idiotic basis of creed alone, in a vast engulfment of barbarity.

"A thousand times more horrible than anything we saw during the war," was the comment of British and Indian officers who watched the blood flow through the East Punjab. "The Sikhs are on the war-path. They are clearing eastern Punjab of Moslems, butchering hundreds daily, forcing thousands to flee westward, burning Moslem villages and homesteads, even in their frenzy burning their own, too." Threatened Moslems assembled on roofs and beat gongs and drums to summon aid. "The Sikhs attack scientifically. A first wave, armed with firearms, fires to bring the Moslems off their roofs. A second wave lobs grenades over the walls. In the ensuing confusion a third wave goes in with kirpans and spears, and the serious killing begins. A last wave consists of older men, often army pensioners with long white beards, who carry torches and specialize in arson. Mounted outriders with kirpans cut down those trying to flee."

It is discomfiting to find our contemporaries still furiously slicing one another into pieces for the sake of God, just as, for dreary centuries, they have cut and hewed for transubstantiation, a doctrine none could understand; for Islam's caliphic heritage; for the precedence among Christian episcopacies; for predetermination and inescapable sin.

The late Curzio Malaparte recounts that during World War II, in the Fascist republic of Croatia, carved from occupied Yugoslavia, he visited Ante Pavelić, *Poglavnik* or dictator of that ferociously Catholic and anti-Serbian creation. "While he spoke," says the Italian author, "I gazed at a wicker basket on the Poglavnik's desk. The lid was raised and the basket seemed to be filled with mussels, or shelled oysters—as they are occasionally displayed in the windows of Fortnum and Mason in Piccadilly in London. Casertano [Italian minister to Pavelić] looked at me and winked, 'Would you like a nice oyster stew?' 'Are they Dalmatian oysters,' I asked the Poglavnik. Ante Pavelić removed the lid from the basket and revealed the mussels, that slimy and jelly-like mass, and he said smiling, with that tired good-natured smile of his, 'It is a present from my loyal *ustashis*. Forty pounds of human eyes.' " These were the eyes of Serbian Orthodox believers in the Byzantine rite of Christianity's expression. Partisan friends of mine in 1943 showed me pictures of Orthodox Serbian *četniks*, with skull and crossbone insigne on their furry hats, displaying similar baskets said to be filled with Catholic Croat eyes.

Voltaire, who was deeply affected by the disastrous Lisbon earthquake in 1755, recognized that "men have always clung to the hope of a life to come; a hope, a truth, often accompanied by doubt. Revelation destroyed doubt and replaced it with certainty; but it is frightful to still hear, each day, disputes on the question of revelation; to see Christian society unsociable, divided in one hundred sects on revelation; to see it slander itself, persecute itself, destroy itself for revelation; to make new Saint Bartholomews for revelation; to see it assassinate Henri III and Henri IV for revelation; to behead King Charles I for revelation! Oh God, reveal to us then that man must be human and tolerant."

The Western revelations aspire to afterlife. Matthew tells how even the saints arose from their graves following Jesus' resurrection. The Moslems are given comfort in the splendid passage of their Prophet to a tiered eternity. As the latter lay with Ayesha, his wife, the angel Gabriel knocked on the door and entered, fluttering innumerable wings, guided him to a white horse named Alborak, held his bridle, reassured the nervous steed by promising him a heavenly seat, and led his charge successively to the seven celestial kingdoms of silver, of gold, of precious stones, of emerald, of adamant, of carbuncle and of divine light. But in more Eastern creeds there is less confidence in foreverness.

Regardless of the theology in which he claims to speak, any man who aspires to be God's prophet is a false prophet. Any man who assumes the right to dictate another's faith is himself faithless. And yet, disregarding this simple truth, man insists on his cruel joke. He invents religion to escape from death and slaughters those who disagree. History's ears throb with the screams of those who died for godless gods. And we, in our time, with the aid of mechanical devices, have pursued the cataleptic creed of killing because of differences in faith. Man has not yet learned that he who persecutes in the name of supernal lordliness is wicked beyond redemption by divinity. We have made our world a Babylon—"and in her was found the blood of prophets, and of saints, and of all that were slain upon earth."

SIX

Death by Battle

DEATH'S MASSIVE TRIUMPHS come with famine, pestilence and war, and of these the last, man-made, is wicked. Some men stand up well to war and die with grandeur. For them it is easier to meet their maker proudly with a weapon. Said La Hire before each battle, that brave and simple captain to Joan of Arc: "Sire Dieu, I pray you to do for La Hire what La Hire would do for you, were you captain-at-arms and he God."

Sometimes, in war, death crawls heavily like a tortoise and sometimes it slinks softly in the night but generally it flourishes with furious passion. Death in battle is sounded by cries, by brass horns, steel clashes, shrieks, whines, by explosions so immense they cannot be heard by those they immolate, by the snick of knives

and by drumbeats, always drums, the dismal drums.
Death is smeared with red and scabby brown blood; it
is dun colored and khaki, covered with dirt and grease;
it is the white of snipping doctors and the black of sad
crows wheeling over the terrible field of Kossovo and
off to Tsarina Milica with the news of her slaughtered Serbs: "Thy lord, the glorious Tsar Lazar . . .
thy father, Jug-Bogdan . . . his eight Jugović sons including Bočko . . . Strahinia Banović . . . Miloš, fallen
on the bank of the icy-watered Silnica, Miloš who
slew the Turkish sultan Murad . . ."

Youth marches off with confidence to war. And
youth comes back lashed belly-down across a mule,
bobbing stiffly as the animal walks. "The first one
came early in the morning. They slid him down from
the mule and stood him on his feet for a moment. . . .
Then they laid him on the ground in the shadow of
the stone wall alongside the road. I don't know who
that first one was. You feel small in the presence of
dead men and you don't ask silly questions . . ."

War produces intense individual concentration, a
trance. The Welsh hero Peredur stood amidst battle
and compared the blackness of the raven, the white-
ness of the snow and the redness of the blood to the
hair of the lady whom best he loved, which was
blacker than the raven, to her skin, which was whiter
than snow, and to the red upon her cheeks, which was
redder than the blood upon the snow appeared to be.
And, so musing, he accepted twenty-four charges by
twenty-four knights, including his enemy Sir Kai,

and hurled each to the ground with a single lance thrust, finally riding over Sir Kai's body twenty-one times without ever disturbing the train of his meditation.

For cruel and bitter people war is a fine experience. Genghis Khan said: "The greatest joy a man can know is to conquer his enemies and drive them before him. To ride their horses and take away their possessions. To see the faces of those who were dear to them bedewed in tears, and to clasp their wives and daughters in his arms."

War has a thousand different aspects. At Hastings the Norman horsemen rode up a slope already strewn with corpses. Leading them was a minstrel named Taillefer, who galloped forward cheering and juggling his sword, casting it into the air and catching its hilt as it spun downward. He burst through the wall of Saxon shields and into the line of King Harold's spearmen, where he was slain after cutting down several opponents. Behind him came the whole Norman knighthood, chanting battle songs.

Duke William himself led charge after charge and had three horses killed beneath him. But the Saxons could not be scattered while their king survived and their standards still fluttered. Finally arrows settled the day. William bade his archers shoot a high trajectory, so that the shafts fell all over the enemy array. One struck Harold in the eye, producing a mortal wound. The arrow shower, combined with the news of their king's fall, broke up the English host. A band of Norman knights thrust in and hewed Harold to pieces as he lay wounded at the foot of his banners. They cut down the Dragon of Wessex and the Fighting Man with guttural shouts, the whinnying of horses and the clash of steel on steel.

The army of the Mongol khan that clattered toward medieval Europe was as numerous as ant swarms. His warriors were reputed brave as lions, immune to the fatigues and hardships of war. They knew neither ease nor rest, flight nor withdrawal. Whithersoever they went, they carried everything they needed, satisfying their hunger with dried meat and sour milk, eating the flesh of any animal, even dogs and swine. They opened veins in their horses and drank the blood. And when the Mongols conquered, they left nothing alive, ripping the bellies of women with child. No mountain or river arrested their brutal progress. They crossed ravines and swam their horses over rivers, holding on to the manes and tails.

At approximately the same epoch, Joinville tells of King Louis's French crusade against the Saracens. His army sickened: "You must know that we ate no fish the whole Lent but eelpouts, which is a gluttonous fish, and feeds on dead bodies. From this cause, and from the bad air of the country, where it scarcely ever rains a drop, the whole army was infected by a shocking disorder, which dried up the flesh on our legs to the bone, and our skins became tanned as black as the ground, or like an old boot that has long laid behind a coffer. In addition to this miserable disorder, those

affected by it had another sore complaint in the
mouth, from eating such fish, that rotted the gums,
and caused a most stinking breath. Very few escaped
death that were thus attacked." Nevertheless, despite
this disaster, a knight named Faracataic, "seeing the
sultan dead, cut him in twain, and tore the heart from
his body. On coming to the king with his hands all
bloody, he said: 'What wilt thou give me who have
slain thine enemy, who, had he lived, would have
put thee to death?' But the good king St. Louis made
no answer whatever to this demand."

Death, dressed in battle, engulfed Cortés's stoutest
soldiers with cruel fanaticism in the green swelter of
Mexico, above which, in the Aztec fort, there sounded
the terrible drumbeats and the terrible shell trumpets.
One of the Spanish dons "looked towards the lofty
cue where they were being sounded" and saw
Spaniards whom the Aztecs had captured when they
defeated Cortés being carried up the steps. "The
Aztecs were taking them to be sacrificed. When they
got them up to . . . where their accursed idols are kept,
we saw them place plumes on the heads of many of
them and with things like fans in their hands they
forced them to dance before Huichilobos, and after
they had danced they immediately placed them on
their backs on some rather narrow stones which had
been prepared as places for sacrifice, and with stone
knives they sawed open their chests and drew out
their palpitating hearts and offered them to the idols
that were there, and they kicked the bodies down the

steps, and Indian butchers who were waiting below cut off the arms and feet and flayed the skin off their faces, and prepared it afterwards like glove leather with the beards on, and kept those for the festivals when they celebrated their drunken orgies, and the flesh they ate in *chilmole*."

Ziska, the great general of the Bohemian Hussites, who made of scythe-wheeled carts a kind of tank, led his forces against those of the Roman Catholic Church and emperor beneath a chalice standard, ravaging the Catholic countryside and burning villages. In his old age, blind and bitter, he was extraordinarily cruel. He used to feel the heads of prisoners, and whenever his groping fingers detected the tonsure of a popish priest he smashed the man's skull with a heavy hammer. Ziska practiced the savage art of war with the fervor of a religious fanatic. When he lay dying he ordered his officers to make a drum of his skin so that its thundering roll would scatter the enemies of his Protestant God.

War has brought cruel death under every famous civilization since the Hittites raped their way across the Anatolian plain and the hosts of Sennacherib swept down to the Mediterranean. Livy tells of the great Carthaginian victory over Rome: "The carnage . . . was a ghastly sight even for the enemy. There all those thousands of Romans were lying, infantry and cavalry indiscriminately as chance had brought them together in the battle or the flight. Some covered with blood raised themselves from amongst the dead

around them, tortured by their wounds which were
nipped by the cold of the morning, and were promptly
put an end to by the enemy. Some they found lying
with their thighs and knees gashed but still alive;
these bared their throats and necks and bade them
drain what blood they still had left. Some were discovered with their heads buried in the earth, they had
evidently suffocated themselves by making holes in
the ground and heaping the soil over their faces. What
attracted the attention of all was a Numidian who
was dragged alive from under a dead Roman lying
across him; his ears and nose were torn, for the
Roman with hands too powerless to grasp his weapon
had, in his mad rage, torn his enemy with his teeth,
and while doing so expired."

This desperate phenomenon, the use of nature's
rudimentary weapons, still occurs. I have myself seen
its scars in the Acroceraunian Mountains that link
Albanian and Greek Epirus. During the autumn of
1940, when a badly-commanded, unenthusiastic army
of Italians invaded Greece, the shock troops opposing them were the famous *Evzones*, an elite corps
usually employed as guards outside the royal palace
in Athens, where, dressed in white kilts, tasseled caps
and pompon slippers, they are much photograghed by
tourists. As commando fighters, nevertheless, they
were famous, attacking behind their battlecry of
"Aera," in effect, "make way for the wind," or creep-
ing over thorn thickets at night on blankets spread

before them to deaden the crackling noise of their advance.

Such expeditions against Fascist outposts were confined to knife fighting, silent murder or the taking of prisoners. When the knife stuck between Italian ribs, the Evzone would use his teeth. I saw pathetic prisoners from Apulia with bad throat wounds that looked as if they had been caused by dogs. One day, in an Epirote outpost, two smiling Greeks in Evzone battledress approached me on hearing I was American. They presented me with a souvenir, a postcard picture of themselves, standing with arms across each other's shoulders, smiling into the camera. On the back was written: "To our American friend from the Evzones, Janni Pappas and Niko Androulis, who are brave Greek soldiers and keep their teeth sharp with Kolynos toothpaste."

Herodotus recounts how earlier Greek heroes crippled an invading horde—a horde of Persians—in the narrow Thermopylae pass. "The barbarians under Xerxes began to draw nigh; and the Greeks under Leonidas, as they now went forth determined to die, advanced much further than on previous days, until they reached the more open portion of the pass. . . . Now they joined battle beyond the defile, and carried slaughter among the barbarians, who fell in heaps." The Persian captains, armed with whips, lashed their men forward. "Many were thrust into the sea, and there perished; a still greater number were trampled to death by their own soldiers; no one heeded the dying. For the Greeks, reckless of their own safety and desperate, since they knew that, as the mountain had been crossed, their destruction was nigh at hand, exerted themselves with the most furious valor against the barbarians.

"By this time the spears of the greater number were all shivered, and with their swords they hewed down the ranks of the Persians; and here, as they strove, Leonidas fell fighting bravely, together with many other famous Spartans, whose names I have taken care to learn on account of their great worthiness, as indeed I have of those of all the three hundred. There fell too at the same time very many famous Persians: among them, two sons of Darius. . . .

"Thus two brothers of Xerxes here fought and fell. And now there arose a fierce struggle between the Persians and the Lacedaemonians over the body of Leonidas, in which the Greeks four times drove back the enemy, and at last by their great bravery succeeded in bearing off the body. This combat was scarcely ended when the Persians with Ephialtes approached; and the Greeks, informed that they drew nigh, made a change in the manner of their fighting. Drawing back into the narrowest part of the pass, and retreating even behind the cross wall, they posted themselves upon a hillock, where they stood all drawn up together in one close body, except only the Thebans. The hillock whereof I speak is at the entrance of the straits, where the stone lion stands which was set up in honor of Leonidas. Here they defended themselves to the last, such as still had swords using them, and others resisting with their hands and teeth; till the barbarians, who in part had pulled down the wall and attacked them in front, in part had gone round and now encircled them upon every side, overwhelmed and buried the remnant which was left beneath showers of missile weapons."

Judas Maccabeus, the greatest Jewish general, met a similar heroic end before the forces of Bacchides, governor of Mesopotamia and general to the Seleucid ruler Demetrius. Behind their trumpeters, both armies charged and the battle continued until sunset. Judas saw that Bacchides and the strongest part of his army were on the right wing and attacked there with his most courageous men, breaking the enemy ranks and driving them backward. He pursued them as far as a mountain called Aza; but when the left wing saw its right had been put to flight, Judas was surrounded and, "being not able to fly, but encompassed round about with enemies, he stood still, and he and those that were with him fought; and when he had slain a great many of those that came against him, he at last was himself wounded, and fell, and gave up the ghost, and died in a way like to his former famous actions. When Judas was dead, those that were with him had no one whom they could regard, but when they saw themselves deprived of such a general, they fled. . . . And this was the end that Judas came to. He had been a man of valour and a great warrior."

The novelists of war have tended to view death's

panoramic carnage through the eyes of a single character. Thus Tolstoy saw Borodino: "The fearful spectacle of the battlefield, heaped with dead and wounded, in conjunction with the heaviness of his head, the news that some twenty generals he knew well were among the killed or wounded, and the sense of the impotence of his once mighty army, made an unexpected impression on Napoleon, who was usually fond of looking over the dead and wounded, proving thereby, as he imagined, his dauntless spirit. . . . He hastened away from the field of battle and returned to Shevardino. With a yellow, puffy, heavy face, dim eyes, a red nose, and a husky voice, he sat on a camp stool, looking down and involuntarily listening to the sounds of firing. With sickly uneasiness he awaited the end of this action, in which he considered himself the prime mover, though he could not have stopped it. The personal, human sentiment for one brief moment gained the ascendant. . . . He imagined in his own case the agonies and death he had seen on the battlefield. The heaviness of his head and chest reminded him of the possibility for him too of agony and death."

Stendhal examines Waterloo through the mind of an inexperienced youth. "Fabrizio's face, pale by nature, assumed a markedly green tinge; the *cantinière*, after looking at the dead man, said, as though speaking to herself: 'That's not one of our Division.' Then, raising her eyes to our hero, she burst out laughing. 'Aha, my boy! There's a tidbit for you!' Fabrizio sat frozen. What struck him most of all was the dirtiness of the feet of this corpse which had already been stripped of its shoes and left with nothing but an old pair of trousers all clotted with blood. 'Come nearer,' the *cantinière* ordered him, 'get off your horse, you'll have to get accustomed to them; look,' she cried, 'he's stopped one in the head.' A bullet, entering on one side of the nose, had gone out at the opposite temple, and disfigured the corpse in a hideous fashion. It lay with one eye still open. . . . What horrified him more than anything was that open eye."

Gil, of whom Walter D. Edmonds writes, found at Oriskany, in 1777, a mass of dead militiamen and green-coated regulars. "They lay in queer positions, on their arms, grasping knife or hatchet or musket . . . or else they lay on their backs. . . . A little way along a face struck him as familiar. . . . Gil looked at it curiously before he recognized it for Christian Reall's face. He had been scalped. The top of his head looked flat and red; and the circumcision of the crown had allowed the muscles to give way so that his cheeks hung down in jowls, tugging his eyes open and showing enormous bloody underlids."

Death came to the Alamo by moonlight behind the savage strains of Santa Ana's battle song, "Deguelo," or the "Cut-throat." The Sioux brought it to Custer's men on a hill east of the Little Bighorn, leaving stripped, mutilated bodies. And death struck Shiloh with particular efficiency in the first war we like to call "modern." There, "A young private of the Fourteenth Illinois came up to Lieutenant Colonel Cam, fumbling at his entrails, which were trying to escape through a great slit in his abdomen, made by a passing shell. The slippery intestines kept working through his fingers. 'Oh, Colonel, what shall I do?' he pleaded. Cam laid him gently behind a tree, whipped tears off his own cheeks, then walked back to the killing. Johnson, an officer of the same regiment, spurred his horse after an elderly Confederate officer, shot him through the body, reached out and seized his victim by the hair. To his horror the whole scalp came off as the Southerner slipped dead from the saddle. A roar of laughter arose above the battle clash and Johnson saw that he held a wig. . . .

"When the lightning flashed the wet and weary Confederates saw sickening sights all around them—naked, bloating flesh, ghastly white faces—and they heard the moaning refrains, 'Water! Water!' in the storm. A. H. Mecklin, a bible student who had joined a Mississippi regiment, thought he heard wild hogs in the bushes. 'Through the dark I heard the sound of hogs quarreling over their carnival feasts.' "

Death engulfed thousands at Ypres during World War I. "I entered one pillbox during the day and found eighteen dead Germans inside. There was not a mark on one of them; one of our heavy shells had made a direct hit on the top of it and they were killed by concussion, but very little damage had been done to the pillbox."

In the Second Great War, from Stalingrad to Ala-
mein, from the White Sea to New Guinea and from
Viipuri to Nagasaki, death used an ever-increasing
arsenal of weapons. It created mass German graves at
Yelnia and mass Russian graves at Kiev. It brought
famine to Leningrad, together with a black market in
rats, cats and human flesh. It whistled through
blacked-out London, sputtered across the Cyrenaican
sand dunes and ratcheted through the Ruhr. At night,
outside the Abbey of Monte Cassino, it cut down
Gurkhas in sheets of Schmeisser fire as they shouted
their knife-fighting cry: "Here are the Gurkhas; take
out your knives!" It thundered in tank attacks, artillery bombardments and the horrendous flooding of
the Hamburg anti-aircraft shelters, smashed by concentrated blockbusters.

But even this was vaguely reminiscent of the past
—the knives of Marathon and Ivry, the shots of
Gettysburg and Sedan, the cannonading of Madrid
and Waterloo, the tanks of the Aisne and the aircraft
at the Second Marne. Death's most impressive battle
contribution came as a nuclear flash in the daylit
sky of Hiroshima during the summer of 1945.

To some Japanese this "seemed a sheet of sun."
Others heard an immense thunder. Rooms were
filled with "blinding light." Refugees, fleeing the city
after this cataclysmic bolt, "met hundreds and hundreds . . . every one of them seemed to be hurt in
some way. The eyebrows of some were burned off
and skin hung from their faces and hands. Others,

because of pain, held their arms up as if carrying something in both hands. Some were vomiting as they walked. Many were naked or in shreds of clothing. On some undressed bodies, the burns had made patterns—of undershirt straps and suspenders and, on the skin of some women (since white repelled the heat from the bomb and dark clothes absorbed it and conducted it to the skin), the shapes of flowers they had had on their kimonos. Many, although injured themselves, supported relatives who were worse off."

A Catholic priest saw "about twenty men, and they were all in exactly the same nightmarish state: their faces were wholly burned, their eyesockets were hollow, the fluid from their melted eyes had run down their cheeks. (They must have had their faces upturned when the bomb went off; perhaps they were anti-aircraft personnel.) Their mouths were mere swollen, pus-covered wounds, which they could not bear to stretch enough to admit the spout of the teapot [the priest bore]. So Father Kleinsorge got a large piece of grass and drew out the stem so as to make a straw, and gave them all water to drink that way."

A child wrote in a school essay: "The day before the bomb, I went for a swim. In the morning, I was eating peanuts. I saw a light. I was knocked to little sister's sleeping place. When we were saved, I could only see as far as the tram. My mother and I started to pack our things. The neighbors were walking around burned and bleeding. . . . We went to the park. A whirlwind came. At night a gas tank burned and I saw the reflection in the river. We stayed in the park one night. Next day I went to Taiko Bridge and met my girl friends Kukuki and Murakami. They were looking for their mothers. But Kukuki's mother was wounded and Murakami's mother, alas, was dead."

Wars, says Burton, "are begun by the persuasion of a few debauched, hair-brain, poor, dissolute, hungry captains, parasitical fawners, unquiet Hotspurs, restless innovators, green heads, to satisfy one man's private spleen, lust, ambition, avarice, etc.; such causes lead folk to accursed battles. Proper men, well proportioned, carefully brought up, able both in body and mind, sound, led like so many beasts to the slaughter, in the flower of their years, pride and full strength, without all remorse and pity, sacrificed to Pluto, killed up as so many sheep, for devil's food, 40,000 at once. At once, said I?—that were intolerable, but these wars last always, and for many ages; nothing so familiar as this hacking and hewing, massacres, murders, desolations. . . . What plague, what fury brought so devilish, so brutish a thing as war first into men's minds? Who made so soft & peaceable a creature, born to love, mercy, meekness, so to rave, rage like beasts, & run on to their own destruction?"

Well might the gloomy philosopher ask. For with its gleaming new atomic armory, death's handmaiden, war, has achieved incalculable prowess and turned us almost to a race of lemmings. Man has always been ingenious in his search for means of killing man. But, until our day, war and death at least were recognizable, within our comprehension: the Spartan mother instructing her son to come back with his shield or on it; the Theban phalanx; the gallant La Hire at Orléans; gay Taillefer juggling his sword; the shivering of spears; the clattering army of the Mongol khans; the thud of Zyska's hammer; the groans of one-eyed Harold; the heaving and panting of the Carthaginians; red-nosed Napoleon queasily looking out on Borodino's carnage; the sweating *conquistadores* of Cortés in steel and cotton-padded armor.

But war, with all its opportunities for heroism, was always death and desolation. From Shiloh to Normandy it became ever more thunderous and mechanical: an echelon of heavy bombers roaring over quaking cities; tanks grinding cowering infantrymen into foxholes with their brutal treads; siege cannon brought to bear from railway trucks upon targets twenty miles away. Yet even all that horrid efficiency has gone with the zebra-striped shields of ancient Crete and Shaka's Zulu *impis*; with the Roman short sword and the English longbow; with Vauban's bayonet and Gatling's multiple gun. War is today a million melted eyes running down flaccid cheeks, vomiting naked armies of civilians and cities obliterated by a sheet of sun. Whatever glamour it once held has vanished. War has become death's finest opportunity to turn this earth into another sightless moon.

SEVEN

Death on a Pale Horse

NOW DEATH has its own special menagerie—the dragons and scaly hippogriffs who draw its chariot, the sweating toads, lizards, slimy snakes and fetid crocodiles. Death has its innumerable insects: tarantulas and scorpions, red ants, poisonous flies, mosquital and mosquitoish bugs; its carnivores; its sea beasts, from the predatory leopard seal to the paralyzing octopus, from the snappish barracuda to translucent hordes of piranha infesting the waters of Brazil.

All through the enormous northern woods are death's symbols, where great slate-colored bodies of water reflect the flat sky and hideous huge pike lie like timber in the weedbeds, peering malevolently at the upper, living world through evil mesozoic eyes. Above, arrowheads of geese thud southward from the arctic tundra belt and ducks scoot frightened across the marshes, wings beating upon frozen air with the shadow of a noise.

Everywhere are the birds of death: the parsee-picking kites of the Indus, Euphrates and the Nile; the ravens of Bokhara; the bald eagle of the Adirondacks; the naked-headed vultures of the Kalahari Desert; the blackbirds who fled bloody Kossovo; the cuckoos, sobbing out Ivo's death to a crenelated town upon the Adriatic, boastful Senj; the magpies, the blinking owls and, farthest south, the lonely, eternally lonely skua gull.

The animal of death, when he approaches on the trail of famine and pestilence, is the pale horse of the Apocalypse behind which follows Hell. This is a shabby, scuffling horse, aged beyond comparison, for famine is death's oldest habit and pestilence his most familiar. When the first cowering men peeped askance from caves they looked for food in rivalry with hunting beasts, often cleverer and better armed. And as they learned to cultivate the vegetation and devour it, fire and flood menaced all their pitiful endeavors. They planted grain and the locusts ate it. They tamed flocks, gobbled by wolves and dogs. Like the Masai in East Africa, they sucked the blood of cattle in constant competition with the tsetse fly. Like the Tartars thundering out of Asia, they opened the veins of ponies and mixed the blood with sour mare's milk until their herds atrophied from thirst or hunger beneath the wheeling, carrion-eating birds of the desert.

Throughout known time bellies have swollen with air and burst in agony, legs have shriveled, necks have gnarled, the paps of women have withered and mewling babies have gasped with pitiful despair. In their fertile valley Pharaoh's Egyptians starved when grasshoppers and floods destroyed their harvests. The Hittites, sipping fermented grain beer through reeds from earthenware pots, hungered when hail storms beat the fields. Desiccated Berbers, dehydrated Arabs, spindle-shafted Hindus and inundated Chinese, bloated with unnutritious shoots and bark beside their savage Yangtze, litter the pages of history.

All the soup kitchens of Bengal could not keep millions from dying during the 1940's when the unbridled greed of merchants hoarded available food. Sir Jagdish Prasad, an Indian official who toured the ghastly province, noted "abandoned children in the last stages of emaciation; men and women who had been without food for so long that they could be fed only after strict medical supervision. Bodies were daily being picked up. . . . A man . . . collapsed on the doorsteps of the Collector's court room. As the body was being removed, a woman huddled in a corner thrust out a bundle and cried, 'Take that also.' It was her dead child." Pandit Godaveris Misra found in the Puri area people "reduced to bags of bones for want of food" who died silently as they sought to nibble wild roots.

Man helps nature manufacture famine. Stalin deliberately starved the peasantry to force submission to his insistence that property be state-owned and state-directed. Across the Ukraine little shawl-draped women and potato-shaped men fought like savages for blades of grass after their crops were stolen by police. Millions died but Stalin won a social victory. He admitted later that it had cost even more lives than victory in World War II, a conflict during which, in Moscow, I saw famished hotel servants furtively stealing crusts. A beggar who approached me one blacked-out snowy night spurned an offer of two dollars' worth of rubles. "What can I do with that?" she snarled. "Give me bread." And in besieged Leningrad, workers' wives stole the carcasses of cats, dogs and rats killed by German shells; human flesh was served as ground meat in the butcher shops.

During Stalin's government-sponsored famine, hunger tortured men until they were no longer men. In the Bashkir republic children were fastened to walls by fathers to prevent them from devouring one another. People ran after farmers like mad tigers, stripping the clothes off their own backs to exchange for bread or a gulp of milk. Ukrainians devoured pigweed, wild oats, clay and sunflower heads, complaining that this diet burned their insides until their stomachs swelled before they died. The Russian writer Irenitskin wrote: "It is a living death. One walks as if always going up hill, and the legs refuse to move under one."

Children were like skeletons, with hollow cheeks, fever-bright eyes and arms and legs like stalks of fennel. "Under the little shirt a swollen stomach sticks out as big as a ripe melon. . . . The child is as still as a tiny corpse dragged out of its coffin."

One American saw a baby's body "stuffed with clay —black, greasy clay called 'eel'—which has no grit and which sticks to the teeth like dough and which stills the gnawing of hunger in the stomach. This substance is beyond the elimination powers of the human system, with the result that it remains in the intestines together with all that follows it. Then comes the swelling of the abused 'innards,' together with masses of worms, and the horrible distension. . . ."

Much of China has always dwelled in hunger's shadow. When the Japanese began to occupy that country in the 1930's they started a wave of destruction that carried on for two decades through war and civil war. The dikes were breached; the great rivers overflowed; and malaria, cholera, kala-azar, plague and typhus swept a famished population. In the southern port of Swatow people staggered to rows of coffins, lined up by Buddhist charities, and lay in them to die. In Chinkiang they huddled in hillside caves, their swollen feet covered with sores, while the women stewed bark, leaves, water and a few grains of rice. Babies were too weak to cry. Locust swarms flew up to add to the accumulating terror.

Famine came to Greece in 1941 behind a clanking Nazi army. The Greeks, cut off from their nourishing free seas, commenced to starve. Women fainted in queues for chickpeas or nonexistent bread. Horses dropped between their wagon shafts and the bodies of abandoned pets littered the alleys of the capital.

By early spring of 1942, Athens, filled with fat Saxons and Bavarians, was losing hundreds of citizens a week and the streets were strewn with the dead and dying. Peddlers carried about little folding tables covered with sweets that sold for the equivalent of a dollar. These sweets were made of beans from the carob tree, usually a pig food, and ersatz cream whitened with marble dust. They produced a great wave of stomach ulcers. In Ommonia Square venders sold sausages of dog, cat and rat meat; ptomaine poison was endemic.

Bodies lay on sidewalks. It was difficult to distinguish corpses from persons who had fainted because of weakness. Passers-by spread handkerchiefs on the faces of those evidently dead. Among these, occasionally, a still form would revive, spit blood into the gutter or crawl to the nearest ground-floor windows, tapping upon them a weak plea for food. Pushcart men, paid by the government, took corpses to the morgue.

Nature produces its special harbingers of famine: flood, hail, sandstorm, drought and ugly swarms of insects that devour all growing things in their path. Year after year, the desert locust sweeps nine million square miles of Africa and Asia, stealing sustenance from human mouths, obscuring the skies and fields with black, clicking greed. A single swarm, flying up from Ethiopia, can contain a billion insects daily eating their own weight and leaving a sinister track behind, breeding while they march.

In the wake of famine comes death's other assistant, pestilence. The Lord God of the Hebrews warned the Pharaoh for whom they slaved: "Now I will stretch out my hand, that I may smite thee and thy people with pestilence."

This toad of pestilence brought to the world in 1347 perhaps the greatest single calamity ever visited upon human beings, Black Death, or bubonic plague. From Constantinople, carried by filthy rodents, it jumped to Greece and to the Greek islands: from Euboea to Hydra and eventually down to Crete; from Cephalonia to Corfu, over the Adriatic into Italy, on to Sicily and southern France. It suppurated into Spain, England, Ireland, spreading to Germany and the Lowlands and even over the Atlantic to Iceland and forbidding Greenland. Europe, from Russia to Portugal to Norway, suffered in its grip. Guy de Chauliac, physician to the Pope at Avignon, said of the epidemic: "I call it great, because it covered the whole world, or lacked little of doing so. . . . It was so great that it left scarcely a fourth part of the people."

Various origins were ascribed to this persistent and continuing curse: the stinks of stagnating water in hot weather; putrid exhalations from the earth; the corruption of unburied carcasses. One year after the spots, buboes, carbuncles and tumors, the stench, the rotting bowels and agonizing vomit had left the Golden Horn, Boccaccio tells us that the plague encompassed the notable city of Florence. "Yet not," he wrote, "as it had done in the East, where, if any bled at the nose, it was a manifest sign of inevitable death; nay, but in men and women alike there appeared at the beginning of the malady, certain swellings, either on the groin or under the armpits, whereof some waxed of the bigness of a common apple, others like unto an egg, some more and some less, and these the vulgar named plague-boils. . . .

"And this pestilence was the more virulent for that, by communication with those who were sick thereof, it gat hold upon the sound. . . . Nay, the mischief was yet greater; for that not only did converse and consortion with the sick give to the sound infection or cause of common death, but the mere touching of the clothes or of whatsoever other thing had been touched or used of the sick appeared of itself to communicate the malady to the toucher."

Death strolled, death bustled, death sauntered, death slunk, death slithered through those gracious medieval towns, burrowing gloomy dungeons, leaping sandstone walls, straddling rivers. It ravaged gleaming Avignon upon its hillside. It furrowed the dour villages of Silesia. It ignored the hardships of Aragon and arid Castile. It stilled the markets of Marseille, Lyon, fat Bruges and the Hansa cities. It emptied the lovely optimistic Gothic churches. It enfolded

the Kutzo-Vlachs, the Wends, the Ghegs, the Mag-
yars, the Saxons and the Tartars of the marshy
Dobrudja. It swept rolling Piedmont, fair France
and the upland English downs. And no one knew
where to flee or how.

"Some there were who conceived that to live
moderately and keep one's self from all excess was the
best defence against such a danger; wherefore, making
up their company, they lived removed from every
other and shut themselves up in those houses where
none had been sick and where living was best; and
there, using very temperately of the most delicate
viands and the finest wines and eschewing all in-
continence, they abode with music and such other
diversions as they might have, never suffering themselves to speak with any nor choosing to hear any
news from without of death or sick folk [as did the
discoursers of the *Decameron* and the participants in
Poe's "Masque of the Red Death"].

"Others, inclining to the contrary opinion, main-
tained that to carouse and make merry and go about
singing and frolicking and satisfy the appetite in
everything possible and laugh and scoff at whatsoever
befell was a very certain remedy for such an ill. That
which they said they put in practice as best they
might, going about day and night, now to this tavern,
now to that, drinking without stint or measure . . .
and with all this bestial preoccupation, they still
shunned the sick to the best of their power."

Cathedral bells tolled incessantly and the gowned

friarly orders shuffled in silence among the dead.
Hooded lepers collapsed still clutching their warning
bells. Bakers fell into their ovens and tillers dropped
in their fields. All order and authority dissolved as
looters, sniffing spices and odoriferous herbs to safeguard themselves while venturing abroad, stole goods
that soon dropped useless from their bloated hands.
Baron, serf, liege, lord, mendicant and mercenary
captain swelled and died. The narrow streets echoed
the funeral pomp of chants as, behind wavering tapers,
the fortunate were carried to their graves. And blood-
suckers called "pickmen" profiteered by pocketing the
pay of pallbearers and dumping bodies in the nearest
alley. Cattle, asses, sheep, goats, swine and fowl
strayed hungrily from untended fields, invading the
untenanted villages of their departed masters.

Time and again this febrile, gangrened, scabrous
death swept Europe. Defoe reported on England's
1665 affliction, when "London might well be said to
be all in tears; the mourners did not go about the
streets indeed, for nobody put on black or made a
formal dress of mourning for their nearest friends; but
the voice of mourning was truly heard in the streets.
The shrieks of women and children at the windows
and doors of their houses, where their dearest relatives
were perhaps dying, or just dead, were so frequent to
be heard as we passed the streets, that it was enough
to pierce the stoutest heart in the world to hear them."

Frightened citizens rushed through the night con-
fessing crimes: "I have been a thief," "I have been an

adulterer," "I have been a murderer." Physicians collapsed while prescribing for their patients. As soon as anyone fell ill, he was locked up in whatever house the illness had struck him and a large red cross was painted upon the bolted door, together with the words "Lord, have mercy upon us." Delirious victims staggered out in bedclothes or, wrapped in blankets, threw themselves into the gaping pits dug as mass graves by the authorities.

Those who went marketing to feed the living touched nothing with their own hands. They used butchers' hooks to handle meat and the butchers in turn dropped their payment into pots of vinegar. Everyone carried perfume against the stench. Only the poor, driven by necessity, showed a certain kind of brutal courage. Whole buildings were filled with whimpering and moans. Infants, numerous times, were discovered sucking the breasts of dead mothers. Naked hysterical men danced giddily through the open streets, followed by supplicating wives who dared not touch them, and those in a frenzied agony of pain were held upon their beds while surgeons burned the swelling flesh with red-hot irons.

"The swellings," wrote Defoe, "which were generally in the neck or groin, when they grew hard and would not break, grew so painful that it was equal to the most exquisite torture; and some, not able to bear the torment, threw themselves out at windows or shot themselves, or otherwise made themselves away, and I saw several dismal objects of that kind.

Others, unable to contain themselves, vented their pain by incessant roarings." And, despite poultices, drawing plasters, leeches and various caustic scarifications, death almost always supervened. Burial hearses became communal.

"The cart had in it sixteen or seventeen bodies; some were wrapt up in linen sheets, some in rags, some little other than naked . . . but the matter was not much to them, or the indecency much to anyone else, seeing they were all dead, and were to be huddled together into the common grave of mankind, as we may call it, for here was no difference made, but poor and rich went together."

Albert Camus imagines an Algerian plague. First, the rats that infested factories and warehouses began to die in batches.

"From basements, cellars and sewers they emerged in long wavering files into the light of day, swayed helplessly, then did a sort of pirouette and fell dead at the feet of horrified onlookers. At night, in passages and alleys, their shrill little death-cries could be clearly heard. In the mornings the bodies were found lining the gutters, each with a gout of blood, like a red flower, on its tapering muzzle; some were bloated and already beginning to rot, others rigid, with their whiskers still erect. . . . You must picture the consternation of our little town. . . ."

Behind the rats came plague. It came with fever, delirium, pain and ganglions, with groans and shrieks. Funeral arrangements became chaotic and few taxis were available to drive mourners to the cemeteries. Church services were soon prohibited. There was a shortage of coffins, of winding sheets, of graveyard space and the "last remnant of decorum went by the board, and men and women were flung into the death-pits indiscriminately."

Death employs as its precursors all manner of hurtful illness. It engenders swellings, taut buboes, clotted lungs, blains. It stimulates the Spanish disease and French disease (each being one and the same), the Baghdad button and the Bassorah boil. It concocts cholera, gyppy tummy and Delhi belly. Its buzzing flies swarm from the cattle of Kilimanjaro and stun human beings with sleeping sickness. It freezes joints and weakens bones, clots arteries, stiffens muscles, clogs intestines, eviscerates kidneys, burns up nerves and causes the strongest men to shiver.

For centuries, throughout the tropics, death followed the insectivorous flight path, spreading as yellowjack or, as the Spaniards called it, "el vomito negro," flushing faces, suffusing eyes, painting tongues and lips bright carmine and turning the skin a jaundiced yellow until, after ceaseless racking vomiting, nothing but black spittle gaggled forth. Death follows the battlefield with typhus germs. Even in our age of boastful hygiene, this insidious fever swept through Poland, East Prussia, the Balkans and into Russia behind the seesawing Nazi and Soviet armies, jumping into neutral Turkey and Iran. And, in its wake, deaths from senility multiplied.

Famine and pestilence travel with disaster—the temblors that ruined Sodom, the floods that lapped the crest of Ararat. Unleashed, those primeval elements, land and water, can produce limitless terror and despair. In 1755, when the great earthquake embraced Lisbon, it was followed by fire, which roared across the ruins to the accompanying noise of groans and howling dogs. Thieves and galley slaves escaped the prisons and plundered the dead. Priests moved silently, hearing confessions and bestowing absolution. One English clergyman, unable to speak Portuguese, was hemmed in by the crowd and baptized by a Catholic priest.

Quakes tore Moroccan Agadir in 1960. "Imagine," said a witness, "that I took you by the shoulders, that I shook you roughly backwards and forwards and then, with a good shove from the side, I made you fall down: that is what this earthquake was to Agadir." Another, imprisoned beneath the rubble for many days, remembered later: "I took my little brother in my arms to cradle him. Armand moaned softly and cried without tears. He begged for a drink, became discontented, then naughty. He began to claw me, then to bite. My sister Jacqueline said to me: 'Armand is dying.' 'If he dies, we die as well,' I answered. Armand, in my arms, quivered, but more and more feebly. He suffered perhaps half an hour, perhaps one day, I have no idea. Then he was quiet and, much later, I felt him all cold against me; I understood then that he was dead."

When Mauna Loa in Hawaii erupted, it shot out zigzagging, dragon-shaped lava rivers that boiled through peaceful villages, ignoring the pigs, herbs and distilled liquor offered in vain propitiation of the ancient gods, before the frightened fisherfolk fled in their canoes. And from the sea great clouds of steam roared forth. As Krakatoa blew up in Indonesia, shaking all of Southeast Asia, tigers and elephants joined herds fleeing to the interior and thousands of monkeys were paralyzed in chattering dread. "The earth is speaking," said a traveler who was present, "and when it speaks man knows only fear."

Pliny the Younger wrote his friend Tacitus about the eruption of Vesuvius in A.D. 79, which Pliny observed from a boat in the Bay of Naples. He wrote of a cloud which hovered over the volcano that it had "shot up a great height. . . . It was at one moment white, at another dark and spotted, as if it had carried up earth or cinders. . . . And now cinders, which grew thicker and hotter the nearer [we] approached, fell into the ships, then pumice-stones too, with stones blackened, scorched and cracked by fire, then the sea ebbed suddenly from under them, while the shore was blocked up by landslips from the mountains. . . . In the meanwhile Mount Vesuvius was blazing in several places with spreading and towering flames, whose refulgent brightness was the darkness of the night set in high relief." Earthquakes, showers of igneous dust, billowing sulphur, vapors and sucking sea noises accompanied these evil phenomena. Meanwhile, the frightened citizens of Pompeii and Herculaneum gathered their togas about them and sought to flee, suffocating in their tracks, preserved for posterity in cruel scoriaceous molds.

Always the thunder of floods, the crash of earthquakes and the rumble of deep, volcanic indigestion, and always accompanied and followed by pestilence and famine. Death single-foots along the land and over the horizon on his pale, apocalyptic steed. From beneath the shadow of this apparition issues an effluence of blank despair. The fields wither; the trees atrophy; the good soil cracks; and the fat maggots of disease flourish within us until, in our fevered dreams, we dream of death's beneficence.

EIGHT

Death by Man's Own Hand

DEATH IS avidly anthropophagous. Since prehistory, men have entertained themselves devising ways to kill one another. The Burmese once trained elephants to tear apart living beings with their trunks, before they trampled them. Indestructible Malone, a minor New York Bowery criminal, was drugged, shot, clad in wet cement and dropped into the Hudson. Manfred, the son of Emperor Frederick, *Stupor Mundi*, hunted humans in the Calabrian marshes and Cesare Borgia, said to have been a Pope's son, is also said to have shot down other humans in the courtyard of the Vatican to test his archer's eye.

Robespierre, a great killer in his day, was taken (at the age of thirty-five) to the Place de la Révolution. He was bounced in a cart, indifferent to the insults of the Parisians he once exhorted. When he arrived at the famous guillotine, although he was wounded, the executioner tore off his bandages, thus wrenching from his stoic silence a shriek of agony. "The blade fell, and the executioner held up the head that the mob might look for the last time on the man who had canonized its virtues and been blind to its faults." Trotsky, another revolutionist indifferent to others' death, was seated in the study of his exile home in Mexico, talking to a man he knew as Jackson. Suddenly there came a ghastly cry. The sixty-year-old Communist tottered out, blood and brain dripping from his impressive head where Jackson (in reality a Spanish hireling of Stalin) had buried an alpenstock. One of Trotsky's many guards sought to assure him that the wound was insignificant. "No," the murdered man replied, "I feel here"—pointing to his heart—"that this time they have succeeded." He dictated his final message: "I am close to death from the blow of a political assassin who struck me in my room. I struggled with him. He had entered the room to talk about French statistics."

Cold Stalin died of stroke, surrounded by trembling henchmen. Mussolini, who had thought of death as noble and almost gay when it applied to others, faced it himself with scant audacity. As he was fleeing northward toward Switzerland, enraged partisans caught him and turned a deaf ear to his pleas and offers of bribes. On his last morning, the Duce sat in shirt sleeves and German military pants, pale, red-eyed, unshaven, in a peasant's house together with his far from ignoble mistress, breakfasting on bread and salami sausage.

Valerio, the tall partisan commander, came for his victims with two khaki-clad guerrillas. They were bustled into a car and driven to a villa surrounded by a wall of rough-hewn stone. There, among flowering trees that opened upon a lake, the Duce was taken from the car. Claretta, his lover, darted before Mussolini with all the fierce possessiveness of Italian women, shouting: "No, he mustn't die!" But they were shoved together and shot at once. The place was marked later with two black crosses erected by a passing knife grinder.

For two hours the bodies lay in the puddled road. Then they were loaded on a truck. One partisan took from Claretta's neck a gold pendant on which was engraved: "Clara, I am you—you are me, Ben." With other corpses they were taken to a garage in Milan where Fascists and Nazis had shot fifteen patriots. As crowds gathered to watch, they were strung up by their heels. His jersey torn and bloodied, his military trousers sodden, his boots split, his face livid, swollen, twisted, his mouth open in death's grimace, the Duce hung like beef. And a great shout went up, recalling the applause that had greeted his appearance in grander, earlier days.

When the news of Mussolini's death reached Hitler one day after the event, the German dictator resolved to shoot himself. He signed a political testament an-

nouncing that he "preferred death to cowardly abdi-
cation or even capitulation." Then, sheltering in a
massive concrete bunker while the rest of Berlin was
being methodically blown apart, he prepared to do
precisely what he once boasted he would never do—
to seek the escape of a coward, avoiding responsibility.

First he had his Alsatian bitch destroyed. Then he
assembled his staff and silently shook their hands.
His chauffeur and his batman were put in charge of
bringing forty gallons of gasoline in jerrycans from a
depot in the battered chancery garden. Hitler summoned his newly-married wife, Eva. They bade farewell to the evil Dr. Goebbels and Martin Bormann
and retired to the Führer's quarters. One report
sounded. Those who opened the door found Eva dead
of poison and a blood-soaked Hitler, shot in the
mouth. The corpses were wrapped in blankets and
taken to a slight depression dug in sandy soil, where
fuel was poured upon them. They burned like torches
when SS Adjutant Guensche set them alight. The
next day Goebbels poisoned his children, shot his wife
and himself and was also burned. Russian troops
burst in later and found the badly charred remains.
All around, the wreckage of Europe's terrifying capital
crumbled, roared, crackled and burst apart in its
lugubrious Götterdämmerung.

In ordinary society and in ordinary times, criminals
are caught and executed. This is an unpleasant and
immoral aspect of what we call civilization. Nevertheless, legal murder is hallowed and approved and the

profession of state assassin is respected if not honored. Such axe men and rope men as Calcraft and Jack Ketch were esteemed by the masses and even William Boilman, who disemboweled traitors alive and stewed their entrails, obtained a certain furtive popularity.

Sir Edward Coke, that forthright, brilliant lawyer of seventeenth-century England, took pains to specify just how the crown should treat the crime of treason. The convicted man "shall . . . be drawn to the place of execution . . . as being not worthy any more to tread upon the earth whereof he was made: also for that he hath been retrograde of nature, therefore is he drawn backward at a horse-tail. And whereas God hath made the head of man the highest and most supreme part, as being his chief grace and ornament, he must be drawn with his head declining downward, and lying so near the ground as may be, being thought unfit to take the benefit of the common air. For which cause also he shall be strangled, being hanged up by the neck between heaven and earth, as deemed unworthy of both. . . . Then he is to be cut down alive, and to have his privy parts cut off and burnt before his face."

No matter what the justification, no matter with what relative kindness the deed is done, whether by gas, guillotine, broadsword, electric chair, dagger or rope, man has no moral right to take the life of other men. Legality does not blunt the edge of terror and he who employs the sword of justice should justly perish by it. Dostoievsky tells us that if, at the instant before his execution, a man, however brave, is given the alternative of spending the rest of his days atop a rock with only space enough (like some Stylitic saint) to sit, he would choose this with relief.

Arthur Koestler observes: "There is indeed a Kafkaesque horror attached to an execution, which goes beyond the mere fear of death or pain or indignity. It is connected not with the brutality but with the macabre, cold-blooded politeness of the ceremony, in which the person whose neck is going to be broken is supposed to collaborate in a nice, sensible manner, as if it were a matter of a minor surgical operation. It is symbolized in the ceremonial handshake with the executioner [not an American eccentricity, thank Heavens]; it is present in the delinquent's knowledge that in the embarrassed stares of the officials he is already mirrored as a dead man with a blue face and ruptured vertebrae; and that what for him is the final, violent termination of life, is for them merely an unpleasant duty, followed by a sigh of relief and a plate of bacon and eggs."

To this one might append a tale of the Spanish civil war. From their cell on the wintry Castilian plain of Cuenca, a group of Nationalists was driven by truck to the distant killing ground. "Aiee, Aiee," shivered a tattered prisoner, huddling against the wind. "*You* think it's cold," said the guard as they bumped into the frozen dawn. "*You* think it's cold? *We* have to ride back again."

Death seizes the good and noble quite as malevolently as it deals retribution to the bad. Jan Masaryk, the jolly democrat who sought to save Czechoslovakia from Communism, was murdered in March, 1948. His assassins tried to make it appear that this lusty *bon viveur*, who liked to cook lucullan meals, discuss philosophy and women, had jumped from the window of Prague's Foreign Office. Later the French Intelligence Service carefully established such was not the case. Masaryk had been shot in the back of the neck and hurled to the pavement of the Czernin Palace by Communist thugs.

There is the evidence of a certain Dr. Teply who, three months later, died (as it was said) of a "wrong injection" he administered to himself. On March 10, 1948, at 5 A.M. Teply was summoned to the Czernin. In the courtyard, a security agent pulled away a blanket, exposing the remains of Masaryk. The doctor recalled: "I ordered one of the policemen to open the pyjamas and I noticed all over the body traces of blows and scratches that appeared to be marks of violence. After a moment I requested that the corpse be lifted. I saw in the nape of the neck the mark of a wound, probably made by a projectile of 7.65 caliber. All around the wound were traces of scorching, indicating that the shot had been fired from very close range. I don't know whether I reflected to myself or aloud or if the policemen heard. I only know that I thought 'this is infamous, a bestial assassination.' " Teply found the heel bones of the murdered man had not, indeed, been fractured by his fall but had been beaten "repeatedly with a very heavy instrument, for example a hammer." He noted marks that revealed how the Foreign Minister had fought, and on the window sill from which he had supposedly leaped were telltale signs of struggle on death's threshold.

Charles Christian Wertenbaker, a good man, found death with difficulty and great pain. He was finally aided across its threshold by his loyal and loving wife. On his final night "the cancer seemed to rouse and to fight him, as if evil were fighting for its own life, which would die with his. I started pumping morphine into him, cutting my fingers a little on the glass tubes, I was breaking as fast as I could, so that our blood mingled for an instant, symbol of all love. He was afraid of crying out and waking the children and I begged him to pass out and promised him he would die whatever I had to do. . . . I said, 'I love you I love you please die,' and he said that one phrase, too, and went into the final struggle to die and did."

Rommel, a great field marshal, was condemned on suspicion of conspiring against the dreadful Hitler. When the SS came for him he told his wife: "They suspect me of having taken part in an attempt to kill Hitler. . . . The Führer has given me the choice of taking poison or being dragged before the People's Court [a process which meant eventual garroting as well as punishment for all his family]. They have brought the poison. They say it will take only three seconds to act." Then, as he took leave, he said to his soldier servant, Aldinger: "I have spoken to my

wife and made up my mind. I will never allow myself
to be hanged by that man Hitler. . . . In about half
an hour there will come a telephone call from Ulm
to say that I have had an accident and am dead."
Twenty-five minutes later the telephone rang. Aldinger answered. He was told: "A terrible thing has
happened. The Field-Marshal has had a haemorrhage,
a brain-storm, in the car. He is dead."

The least cruel murder is self-murder. Western
tradition sees this as a crime although the Bible tells
us Abimelech, Samson, Saul, Ahithophel, Zimri,
Judas and the jailer in Acts all slew themselves.
Nevertheless, Thomas Aquinas proves with severe
logic that this is "the most fatal of sins, because it
cannot be repented of." Protestantism is equally hard
on suicides. And, right into the last century, they
were buried at crossroads, often with a stake through
their hearts.

Why this cruel torment for those who could no
longer bear life's burden? Why this sadistic lack of
pity for those who most required boon? Literature
and romantic history are filled with admired suicides
from Cleopatra to Werther, Ophelia and the brave
Suliot women. Gismunda was buried beside her Guiscardus "so their bodies might lie together in the grave,
as their souls wander about in the Elysian fields."

In the Orient, by contrast, suicide is reckoned sad
but dignified. Indeed, it was approved by the most
complex societies. As long ago as the sixth century

we find reference to the Hindu habit of sati (suttee), by which the widow lay down beside her husband on a pyre and was consumed. "His wife, loyal and loving, beloved and fair, followed close behind him into the flames." The Japanese code of Shinto called for self-destruction by especially painful means for the gentleman remiss in feudal duties. He selected a dirk, regarded it respectfully (and, if others were present, bowed to them). He slipped off upper clothing to expose his middle, wedged kimono sleeves beneath his knees to prevent the indignity of toppling backward, stabbed himself deeply below the waist, slowly drew the knife from left to right and turned it in the wound, allowing no murmur on his lips nor any expression on his face. This manner of passing through death's portal is still by no means unknown in Japan, where the forty-seven noble *Ronin*, after taking vengeance on an unjust lord by craft and violence, atoned with the customary seppuku (or hara-kiri), winning perpetual devotion and a simple, common grave in Tokyo.

Only for defense or hunger can one justifiably kill another than oneself: to protect one's loved ones or to stave off famine—even if the taste of human flesh is currently démodé. I know a man who claims to have assisted at a feast of "long pig," a dish once widely popular in Polynesia and Melanesia. He pronounced it pleasing to the palate. At Korolevu in the Fijis I asked a huge and friendly fisherman how such flesh tasted to his cannibal ancestors and he nodded approval with a happy smile. Many a New England whaling crew, forced to abandon ship and oar its terrible way, ate weaklings as they died or cheerlessly drew lots and slew and chewed each other.

An interesting constitutional question was posed in the French Ivory Coast in 1950 when Senator Victor Biaka-Boda disappeared into the jungle and was devoured by his constituents. Monsieur Biaka-Boda, a senator elected to the Council of the Republic, took part for several years at Paris and Strasbourg in debates on democracy and European federation. Then he returned to make stump speeches in the bush. All that was ever found of him was a heap of whitened, well-picked bones. These were airmailed to the Ministry of Justice but never formally identified. Since, under the Fourth Republic's law, a man could not be considered legally dead without a proven *corpus delicti,* the voters of Biaka-Boda's district were for long disfranchised. One may reflect: you can't eat your senator and have him too.

The sub-Saharan Bangwa, at the end of the nineteenth century, were most splendid and advanced cannibals. Their chiefs wore belts of hippopotamus hide, studded with knives and nails. Their headdresses were of monkey skins and the plumage of colored birds. They smeared their bodies with palm oil and their faces with red paint. And they devoured their enemies with gusto for the spiritual reason that they hoped to acquire new virtues from the brave dead and for the physical reason that they were often hungry.

One observer, at the time, reported: "I have seen the wild, exciting feast, where spirit dances and invocations have been the principal items, and I have seen the warriors in all soberness sit down to a 'joint of man' in exactly the same way as they would do to a piece of forest antelope. Once, when told by a European that the practice of eating human flesh was a most degraded habit, the cannibal answered, 'Why degraded? You people eat sheep and cows and fowls, which are all animals of a far lower order, and we eat man, who is great and above all, it is *you* who are degraded!' "

I think one can protest with cogency that man, when he produces death for other men, can do so with a modicum of justice only in the name of famine or defense. Such killing nourishes life for dear ones or oneself. And man-made death by any other logic is without excuse. Nor is there any justice in the Mosaic law of eye for eye, tooth for tooth and life for life. What is the punishment for a one-eyed man who half blinds his normally-visioned enemy?

I am minded of Ivan Ivanov, the faithful Bulgarian peasant who earned his reward from God. God said to him: "Ivan, my son, you have been so fine a peasant that I shall honor you by doing anything you want. Only remember, in the name of generosity, whatever I do for you, I shall do twice as much for your neighbor across the river, Jovan Jovanović, the Serb." Ivan thought a while, removed his sheepskin cap and scratched his head. "Lord," said he, "so be it. Take out one of my eyes."

Murder is no excuse for murder nor can justice ever be rendered with the knife. This is a problem for the morality of man. Death, the great anthropophagite, is indifferent to the means of its accomplishment. Gentle, banal, brutal, feverish or calm, it is disinterested both in its methods and its clientele.

NINE

The Anatomy of Death

NOW WHAT IS the appearance and the delineation of death? Is he that familiar skeleton, sometimes borne upon a fleshless horse and sometimes striding bonily across the wasteland? Is he an educated elephant tearing apart Burmese nobles as simpering, silk-clad ladies fan themselves? Is he Rasputin, pierced by holes and poisoned, failing to grasp the ice floes of the Neva? Is death Manfred hunting slaves? Is death a Serbian tombstone bearing the plain words: "Killed by the evil-doing hands of the gendarmes"? Or a cross of wood above the Tonto Rim marked: "Three of us killed this son-of-a-bitch"?

Is death the Polish puppet called Goik, carried on horseback and thrown into the duck pond? Is death a *penitente* flagellant in coarse hooded gown, a Shiah

159

mob amid rivulets of blood? Is death a black man hanging from a rope beneath a swamp cottonwood? Is death a serpent, a raven, an asp, a flaming sheet of napalm or an exploding, sun-sized skull? Is death a werewolf leading Peloponnesian peasants up a mountainside at midnight?

Each of us has a limited experience of death but we can draw upon the knowledge of all men to contemplate its meaning. For Shakespeare death was variously a "pale flag," a "black night," "a necessary end," "a drunken sleep," "a lover's pinch," a "fell sergeant," a "lean abhorred monster," "unsubstantial" and "proud." For Burns it was an "untimely frost," "the poor man's dearest friend." For Shelley it was "the veil which those who live call life," a "gulf." For Donne it was "strong and long-liv'd."

Tranquil Sir Thomas Browne saw death as "the cure of all diseases" and "This reasonable moderator and equal piece of justice." For the various authors of the Bible death had different attributes. It could "flee," it had a "dominion," it bore a "sting," it possessed "sharpness" and it rode "a pale horse."

Longfellow saw death both as "the consoler" and "a Reaper." For Francis Thompson it was "pontifical" and a "rotten" dunger of "harvest-fields." Dryden conjectured that "death, in itself, is nothing." He also conventionally saw in it "the journey's end." Rossetti ascribed to death both "desultory feet" and an "imperishable wing."

For Gray death had a "dull cold ear." For Wordsworth it was a "skeleton." For Beddoes it was a "dotard" and bore "asses' ears." Masefield considered it "grand" and an opener of "unknown doors." It was Rupert Brooke's "worst friend and enemy" but Spenser's "end of woes." Nicholas Rowe thought it "the privilege of human nature" and Samuel Johnson "kind Nature's signal of retreat."

Herbert could see death "working like a mole." Whitman found it "lovely . . . soothing . . . delicate . . . cool-enfolding." For Keats it was "easeful" and for Henley an "old nurse" with "friendly and comforting breast." Chesterton could imagine its being drunk "like wine at Austerlitz." For Webster (who, as Eliot later wrote, "was much possessed by death") it "hath ten thousand several doors." Tennyson saw it endowed with "jaws" and shaped like a "valley." Sir Walter Scott could regard it as a "next-door neighbor for so many years" and Sir Walter Raleigh as "eloquent, just and mighty." For Kyd it was "lively"; William Morris found it "hated" because uncomprehended; the eighteenth-century Edward Young considered it a leveler which "joins us to the great majority"; and the cocky Tommies of World War I prayed that it was personally avoidable: "The bells of Hell go ting-a-ling-a-ling for you but not for me."

Many have written of man's relationship to death. La Fontaine observed: "Death never takes the wise man by surprise; he is always ready to go." John Donne dolorously remarked: "Any man's *death* diminishes *me,* because I am involved in Mankind."

And Francis Bacon, in his noble essay "On Death," said comfortingly: "I do not believe that any man fears to be dead, but only the stroke of death. . . . Men fear death as children fear to go in the dark; and as that natural fear in children is increased with tales, so is the other. . . . There is no passion in the mind of man so weak, but it mates and masters the fear of death. . . . Revenge triumphs over death; love slights it; honor aspireth to it; grief flieth to it. . . . Death has this also, that it openeth the gate to good fame, and extinguisheth envy."

What is this ass-eared, slow-footed, horse-borne, arrogant, skeletal, pontifical, comfortable-breasted, fearsome, friendly figure death? It approaches with the daintiness of a greyhound and it approaches with the force of a bull rhinoceros. It is cunning and it is blind. The smell of death is slightly sweet; its taste is rancid; its sound comes forth in gasps and rattles; its touch is cold; and its sight is changeable: first tranquil beauty that removes life's lines and then corruption followed by clean bones and dust.

I have seen death stalk across central Russia's cold white slopes, harvested with bodies lying stiffly in the winter sun, blood frozen crimson to their wounds. I have seen death in the Rapido Valley, stamped on the faces of young Americans sprawled in the mud amid the flotsam of their love letters, their throats entirely eaten out by scavenging dogs of war. And I have seen death walk hesitatingly down the streets of burning Salonika. There death was frail: a tiny old man bearing a cardboard box. The bombs dropped; along the waterfront the buildings crackled; and terrified Hungarian dancing girls, their lips still smeared with stale lipstick, came running from their interrupted sleep. The bodies of children lay iced in the final attitudes of play. And death came walking: a tiny old man with green complexion, sprouting beard and the half-closed eyes of a hypnotic, walking along and picking up clots of flesh to fill his cardboard box; just like a rubbish gatherer in a public park.

Death is a fish thrown flopping on the beach. Death is a night wolf running through the fog. Death is a cypress grove around a silent Mediterranean cemetery. Death is a wailing wildcat. Death is a little mink nibbling a pike with little teeth. Death is a sleeping ram; a sphinx.

For Sergey Golovin, the Russian terrorist, death was "something incidental and foreign." Death is a small thing, the quantity of a hazelnut, lying on the hand of Princess Radziwill. Death is the Buddha, given over to austerities, sitting cross-legged in the Sarnath deer park.

Death closes his own eyes and disposes his own body, creating a picture that requires not the slightest alteration by those who would come and shroud it. Death is the aridity and emptiness of the night of desires. Death is a weariness of this life and an over-earnest desire for the next, which is not. Death is an Irish peat bog, black as coal, where speckled fish leap and the cuckoo calls its hollow call. Death is a dismal seat in Hell upon a serpent's knee. Death is the Hindu husband, mad with wine, saying "Byom, Byom" beside the corpse of his wife.

Death has its own runes and signs. Here

is the death of one child.

And here is death's destruction and disorder.

Here is the triceps of eternity.

And here is the inverted cross where Peter died.

Here is St. Andrew's death.

Here is death by poison

and here is Yew, death's own private rune.

Poe contemplated death in many forms. The Red Death came "like a thief in the night" and with "darkness and decay . . . held illimitable dominion over all." Death was also a black cat walled inside a tomb, a "hideous beast whose craft had seduced me into murder, and whose informing voice had consigned me to the hangman." For Poe death had a terrible and "suspiciously lingering smile."

Dostoievsky was touched by the death of children. "Ilusha," he writes, "lay with his hands folded and his eyes closed in a blue coffin with a white frill round it. His thin face was hardly changed at all, and strange to say there was no smell of decay from the corpse. The expression of his face was serious and, as it were, thoughtful. His hands, crossed over his breast, looked particularly beautiful, as though chiselled in marble."

Hemingway keenly studied death. He notes that "Until the dead are buried they change somewhat in appearance each day. The color change in the Caucasian races is from white to yellow, to yellow-green, to black. If left long enough in the heat the flesh comes to resemble coal-tar, especially where it has been broken or torn, and it has quite a visible tar-like iridescence. The dead grow larger each day until sometimes they become quite too big for their uniforms, filling these until they seem blown tight enough to burst. The individual members may increase in girth to an unbelievable extent and faces fill as taut and globular as balloons."

He discovered "The first thing that you found out about the dead was that, hit badly enough, they died like animals. Some quickly from a little wound you would not think would kill a rabbit. They died from little wounds as rabbits die sometimes from three or four small grains of shot that hardly seem to break the skin. Others would die like cats, a skull broken in and iron in the brain, they lie alive two days like cats that crawl into the coal bin with a bullet in the brain and will not die until you cut their heads off. Maybe cats do not die then, they say they have nine lives, I do not know, but most men die like animals, not men. . . ."

166

When mass-produced and unexpected, death always leaves behind a phantasmagoric litter. During London's great seventeenth-century fire, Pepys found "Everybody endeavoring to remove their goods, and flinging them into the river or bringing them into lighters that lay off: poor people staying in their houses as long as till the very fire touched them, and then running into boats, or clambering from one pair of stairs by the water-side to another. And among other things, the poor pigeons, I perceive, were loth to leave their houses, but hovered about the windows and balconys till they were some of them burned, their wings, and fell down."

As the *Titanic* sank it took down with it to death's greedy locker, in addition to a gasping human cargo, the following booty: a jeweled copy of the Rubáiyát, 800 cases of shelled walnuts, 15,000 bottles of ale and stout, 30 cases of golf clubs and tennis rackets, tons of coal, 30,000 fresh eggs, dozens of potted palms, 5 grand pianos, a massive silver duck press, shuffleboard sticks, a 50-phone switchboard, 8 dozen tennis balls, a cask of china for Tiffany's, a case of gloves for Marshall Field, an ice-making machine, a brand-new English automobile and innumerable beautifully packed trunks.

Death at sea invariably leaves its flotsam. Four hours after the *Andrea Doria* sank, bearing my friend Camille Cianfarra with his daughter, pinned in their cabins, I sailed by the bubbling carnage: up-ended rafts, chair splinters, vegetables, bottles, empty bits of clothing. Whenever the Germans used to bomb the Mediterranean ports, quantities of stunned fish rose lethargically to the surface to float with beams and empty bottles among the battered ships and wharves.

If people kill one another with deliberation and not in fits of passion, they often rob the doomed of any chance to die respectfully composed. "The Romans," says Koestler, "deprived their victim of the dignity of death by throwing him to the beasts in the arena with a clown's mask attached to his face; we put a white cap over his head [when hanging him] and if the victim is a woman she is made to put on waterproof underwear on the morning of the execution."

The Nazis were avid students of death in all its attitudes. Himmler chose what he called "arch criminals," usually Jews, Russians or Poles, for experiments at Dachau in a specially equipped mobile laboratory. "The equipment made it possible to simulate conditions during an ascent to high altitudes and during rapid descent. Heart action of the subjects was measured by an electric-cardiograph. Autopsies were conducted immediately upon death ('the blood does not yet boil at an altitude of 70,000 feet')."

Another experiment involved the effect of freezing. The subjects, clothed or stripped, were immersed in chill water until they grew stiff. Their temperature was measured by thermo-electric means. Other prisoners were exposed overnight to sub-zero air. When their screams created too much of a disturbance, anesthesia was sometimes used. According to one eyewitness, it took two Russian officers, immersed naked in ice water, five hours to die. During the third hour a Polish orderly heard one of the Russians say to the other: "Why don't you ask the officer to shoot us!" The second replied it was useless to expect mercy from the Fascist dog.

Skinning tattooed corpses to make lampshades was an eccentricity of certain Nazi executioners. And Eugen Kogon tells us: "Professor Hirt, on his part, late in 1942 suggested to Hitler that a collection of skulls and skeletons of 'Jewish-Bolshevist commissars' be created. The SS Main Economic and Administrative Office immediately instructed Auschwitz to make concentration-camp inmates available for this purpose, and 113 persons were selected—seventy-nine Jewish men, thirty Jewish women, two Poles and two Asiatics. They were shipped to the Natzweiler camp, where they were gassed with cyanide which Professor Hirt gave the Camp Commandant for the purpose."

Sadistic and scientific fascination with death was a peculiarity of the Hitler regime. British Tommies, indeed, used to cut off the ringed fingers of corpses in the Western Desert battlefield or smash out teeth for gold fillings; but only for callous, uncruel reasons of cupidity. The Russians have slaughtered from Katyn to Siberia with impassive and disinterested calm. But the Nazi approach to wholesale death gave that condition an unequaled horror.

With my own eyes I witnessed this in Vienna in

1938 after Hitler had taken over Austria. Aided by an unbalanced American who later became a traitor to his country, Robert Best, I bribed the guardian of the city morgue to lock me in for the night in the huge room that held unclaimed pots of ashes, unclaimed bodies and Teutonically efficient ledgers. The pots, which weighed surprisingly little although they looked like the truncated noses of eight-inch shells, were of a black plastic material. A tin disk was pressed into the top of each on which was stamped the name, birthplace, vital dates and site of death of the victim. All had expired at Dachau, the nearest concentration camp. They were presumably unclaimed because remaining relatives had been exterminated in the interim.

One could peruse the heavy-paged ledgers listing similar statistics for the sheet-covered corpses laid out on wheeled tables. In each instance the cause of death for these was registered as "suicide." But, upon pulling back the sheets and regarding the bodies, one was inclined to doubt that anyone would be so insane as to take his own life by the means evidently employed. People do not beat out their own eyes.

Most artists study the mien of death and dying: the sculptor of Laocoön, the Etruscan effigists, the Burgundian Claus Sluter, Michelangelo, Grünewald, Rembrandt, Dürer, Meissonier. Parrhasius, an Athenian painter, was unsatisfied with his own capacity to express the pains and passions of Prometheus upon his Caucasian rock. Therefore he bought an old slave captured by Philip of Macedon and tortured him to death so he could better examine the human mirror of eternity's brink. Pontormo kept corpses swelling in water troughs to serve as models for his "Deluge."

Goya, among painters, knew death well; Signorelli imagined it and Bosch mocked it. The Christian Counter-Reformation was preoccupied with death because it was intent on mass-producing it; Baroque sculpture, El Greco and the English metaphysicists were sombre and delightful consequences. Beethoven understood its sound and Palestrina suspected its intentions.

But death has innumerable faces, meanings, noises and agonies. It comes on heavy-beating wings to touch the Egyptian first-born. It sucks silently downward into the caverns of the sea. It spreads putrescence on the battlefield. It extends its fungus slowly through rotting bodies. It strikes with sudden clangor or insidious secrecy. Genghis Khan, when it took his favorite son, brought it tearing down an entire Afghan valley, uprooting every living thing, each butterfly, each blade of grass. It arrives in skull pyramids outside Isfahan and Baghdad and in great gulps among snapping Congo crocodiles. Its aspects are as infinite as its implications; for death alone cannot be buried, despite the young girls of medieval Nuremberg who carried a doll symbolizing death in a coffin through the streets, chanting they would drown it. It seizes great dust clouds of goose dung, blonde maidens' hair, coal, bananas, rubies and heroic hearts. It engulfs eels, murderers and hummingbirds.

Death walks like a centipede through green jungles. It sends its vultures to devour Parsee corpses left among the trees along the Indian Ocean. Its quiet tides drift over forests of masts: the triremes, argosies, barks, sampans, clippers, schooners, dhows, dreadnoughts, sambuks, whalers, cutters and catamarans; the galleons, galleasses, galleys and galliots; zabras, frigates, caravels; barkentines, pinnaces, urcas, caïques; carracks, pataches, hoys and crumsters—all splendid ships. Death's clients are placed on pyres, in coffins, sacks and brandy casks, watched by hired sentries through the quiet night. Death picks the bones of dinosaurs and lost aircraft. It sweeps across howling Antarctica, the Hindu Kush and the desert of Kizil Kum. It marches, an army of blind Bulgarians, chained by their captor, Emperor Basil, up to the gates of Ochrid, where Pan once played his pipes and horrified Tsar Samuel hurls himself into its embrace. Its knife cuts the throats of Algerian *égorgés* as once it lifted bloody scalps in old Kaintuck. I have seen death in Venice and death in Burma, death in London, in Zagazig and Volokolamsk. And death's corrupting processes are inevitably ugly and invariably the same. As was written of Fair Rosamund, the mistress of proud Henry II of England:

> She that smelled so sweet of yore
> Smelleth now, but sweet no more.

When death came to the early Chinese Dukes of Chin it approached balefully, replete with magic. Eight huge black birds swooped down on their majestic palace, dancing upon the terrace, while tempests broke the ritual vessels and hurled tiles from the roof.

Farther south, death engulfed the great Khmer empire with the stench of pestilence and the rustle of despair, leaving in its wake the untenanted ruins of Angkor: empty halls, pitted images, stone gods, all covered with bat dung and surrounded by an ever-threatening tangle of vegetation loud with cicadas in the dusk.

The wealth and refinement of the Khmer capital were beyond comparison. Its hunters trapped millions of kingfishers, whose brilliant wings were bought by China to be fashioned into diadems for brides. Caravans and sailing ships bore away from its markets ivory, beeswax and rhinoceros horn. Its monarchs ruled with unparalleled splendor. They wore golden tiaras and twisted their hair into chignons twined with jasmine. Each carried a golden sword and protected himself from assassins with iron armor.

A thirteenth-century Chinese diplomat reported the Khmer sovereign had five wives and three thousand concubines. He commanded a bodyguard of amazons. His mandarins were scented with sandalwood and musk. The *bonzes*, or priests, of Buddhism thronged about in orange robes. Holidays were celebrated with processions of goat-drawn carriages, princes on elephants bearing red parasols, hordes of royal mistresses in gilt palanquins.

Monumental temple sanctuaries were raised in this verdant, steaming area. Each evening the king, called for his white complexion the Leper King, would visit their cool recesses to receive the Snake Queen. If she failed to arrive, it was assumed that he would die. And one day the Snake Queen was detained; and death came as her substitute for all the glory of the Khmers, leaving behind dust and rubbish, the roar of tigers, the harsh cry of elephants, the belling of wild stags, the sound of birds and insects, the leathery flap of bat wings, the almost imperceptible stir of thick undergrowth coiled everywhere like a spring. And everywhere death blotted out, in its mysterious encompassment, the throbbing life of the Khmers in the palaces of Angkor's caress-rotted kings.

All through Asia death has left its ruination, sometimes approaching with the resonance of brass trumpets and bull horns and sometimes scuttling like a lizard through the tall teak forests, scattering before it the fleeing monkeys, sending the ravens cawing above the fetid Javanese temple of Borobudur, dispatching its crows to flap heavily above the tomb of Ulug Beg in Turkestani Samarkand.

Death insinuates; it thunders; it falls like dusk in the sky. It tears with the metal claws of the leopard men in Africa. It rots the fragrant clove trees of Zanzibar, blowing in on the monsoon above the sambuks and dhows. It hollows out the vast sequoias in splendid California. It licks with the tongues of lampreys nibbling Roman slaves. It steals sovereigns like Egyptian Rameses and Spanish Philip, struggling to complete their pompous tombs before they die.

Its panoply embraces each great chieftain of the East: the scrawny Fakir of Ipi, the Sultan of Jogjakarta, known as "He who has the World in his Lap"; the Paku Alam, "Nail of the Earth"; the Obud of Ubud, the Susuhunan of Solo, the Bong of Wong, the Wali of Swat, the Nono of Spiti, the Jamsahib of Las Bellas, the Imam of Yemen, the Shahinshah and Padishah. In the sheepfolds of Mongolia lie the early Mongol princes, and from Lahore and Bokhara to the Golden Horn of Istanbul, behind the Mosque of Suleiman, Sinan's masterpiece, are the bones of their descendants, the pashas, beys and aghas of the Seljuk and Osmanli days, together with the Töpkapi treasure of their sultans, including John the Baptist's withered arm and jewel-encased cranium and Alexander's marble-covered sarcophagus from Sidon, showing beautiful Greeks and Persians dealing each other death.

Ah, what a magnificent line of conquerors, horseborne hordes behind horse-tail standards, trotting out of the Altai and the Tien Shan mountains! "Filthy as demons, devils for savagery, and numerous as the falling raindrops," says Vassaf, the Slavic chronicler, they "rolled in waves across the frozen river with the speed of the wind and of fire. The rattling of their chariots and the clashing of their horses' hoofs were like thunder and lightning. With their wrath in full flame, they advanced."

Of this clangorous assemblage who rode into the Levant and Europe on their little ponies with their camel-carried kettledrums, their clashing apparatus of Bektashis and Yüzbashis and Bashibazooks, only Murad II, that modest, pious Turkish lord of lords, would seem to have recognized platonic truth: "Those who pursue philosophy rightly, study to die." In green and delightful Bursa, citadel of the Seljuks, we still can see his lidless sepulchre, containing the royal body embalmed in sweet earth and sprouting grass, under an open hole in the domed roof so that the rain and other friendly elements can enter, as commanded by the sultan. He wished to lie beneath the skies. And outside, on a huge tree now more than half a millennium in age, pigeons coo serenely as the muezzins call to prayer the shrinking numbers of Islamic orthodox, bearded old men preparing to join Murad.

Certain races, like the Spaniards, have adored death throughout life. Often, after a heavy meal of roasted pig and purple wine, I have sauntered through cemeteries in Segovia and Burgos with distinguished caballeros examining graveyard plots with the keen eye of future tenants.

In Greek Euboea death comes in a rattling bus and bears away a young man lying across his blackgowned mother's lap. Ali Pasha, the Lion of Janina, gave death to his wives in sweetened form. He bound them in sacks and cast them into the serpent-covered lake, first spreading it with sugar.

When Ibn Saud, that patriarchal ruler of Arabia, was a young man, he sneaked out of Kuwait with a handful of retainers and stormed the walls of the desert town of Riadh. The Emir Bin Jiluwi told me of that battle. Saud was wounded in his private parts as he left the storming ladder. Bin Jiluwi mourned for him: "Alas, Abdul Aziz, you can never again enjoy life's greatest pleasure and its meaning." "Bring me a woman," ordered Ibn Saud. They brought a slave girl from a mud house. There, amid the fighting and the burning and the screams, the King proved he was not dead and then they went on to kill, capturing a kingdom in the process. Death never called on Ibn Saud until, old, gnarled and bent, riddled with wounds, infested with disease, sire of an impressive lineage, he expired peacefully in Mecca decades later.

My Italian friend Gino Tomauoli officered in a Bavarian infantry regiment retreating from Kharkov in 1943. The Russians rode out at dawn and dusk each day, firing tommy guns from their horses in the mist; and although each day the Germans mowed them down, each day there were more Russians and fewer Germans. "We kept alive in houses of the dead," says Gino. "The ground was frozen. We could not dig for shelter. So we made lean-tos of the corpses of both armies. We stretched our tents on top as canvas roofs. The wind blew hard against those human walls. The dead protected us from death."

Within the cool Allegheny County morgue, I used

to watch how, on hot noons, the citizens of Pittsburgh brought their sandwich lunches and their children to regard, laid out on medical slabs, covered with white cloths except for medically cosmetic faces, bodies hauled out the night before from factory slums or the flowing Monongahela and Ohio rivers.

I saw death explode from Vesuvius in 1944 and I saw death come to a Tosk peasant, racked with a tubercular cough, in the Albanian village of Vlora while other peasants waited impassively for a bus and children played "the paper game"—flicking a scrap with sticks. And I saw death in the catacombs of Rome when they opened up the tomb of Italian patriots, machine-gunned by the Nazis and then dynamited in. An American colonel who had thought talk of atrocities was propaganda talk vomited on the spot.

The shards of death are often the subject of contention. The world is filled with saintly relics: teeth, hairs, bones and bony fragments, pertaining allegedly to holy men. Corpses have been kidnaped and moved to religious shrines. Corpses have been sold. The needy monks of Athos used to carve them up for auction piecemeal to the autocephalic churches.

It was usual in the Middle Ages, as in the instance of the Cid, to mount the remains of a conqueror upon his horse and tie them there, pretending the general still lived to guide his troops to victory. As late as 1948 Riff leaders kidnaped the body of their hero, Si Abbas, and moved it from Moroccan Fez to Ajdir,

178

massing their tribesmen to repel the king's army when it arrived to steal back the remains.

How various is death's approach. Does it come with a knife? Or the clutch of a rope? Or the rend of a bullet? Or the cool fatigue of water? Or the stench of agonizing cancer? Or the soft stealth of barbiturates? Or the breathless pain of bursting heart and head?

Death has so many remarkable ways of making its presence known. It ranges from the ghastly to the humorous and from the magnificent to the banal. It cannot be compartmentalized and man himself, as he becomes more clever or more audacious, increases the diversity of death's ways.

It comes with disease, with murder, with torture, with famine, with suffering, taking the ancient and the young, the healthy and the frail, the great and the lowly, those who believe in it and those who don't. But often it steals peacefully, embracing those who crave it as a solace from the agonies of life. It strokes fevered brows in bed and accepts tired bodies in its cool repose. My friend Jack MacCormac, on the banks of a Norwegian stream, was playing a large salmon in the quiet evening of his life when he was clasped by kindly death.

Death levels off, indifferently, the killers and the killed. It can be loud and great, as infinitely huge as space, dimension of the future. And death can be silent and infinitely small, equaling infinite littleness, dimension of the past.

We have barely begun to measure either dimension, to know the silence of distance or the noise of the atom as it begrudgingly splits into tinier, ever tinier morsels. As many undiscovered smallnesses are hidden within that atom as there are hidden universes still unseen.

Dimensions are the same to death whether in space or time. Whichever way they stretch we can conceive of them only as an X. Nothing can be measured, neither minute past nor massive future; and the present does not exist. For death does not acknowledge it.

TEN

The Death We Face Within Ourselves

DEATH HAS its special abodes and nowhere in our world can its immensity be contemplated better than on death's own continent, Antarctica. Here are death's silences and also its cacophonous sounds: the bone-cracking noises, crashing glaciers, pulverizing pack, shrieking wind, the dull throb of continual disintegration. Here we view death's spectacle of desolation: ah, how infinite that desolation seems when measured against our standards of experience.

This lean book, larded with the fat of others' works, has been written on four continents, all of which, even the continent holding brilliant Greece, are included in death's bland domain. But Antarctica (where these words are written) is truly death's special terrestrial home. In all history no man has inhabited its gusty vastness in the nonexploratory sense of habitation. There is no inland life removed from the borders of its frozen seas except for the occasional skua gull, the hatching emperor penguin and a wingless fly whose eggs can survive ten thousand years' refrigeration before submitting to extinction. Not even germs live in Antarctica.

Nature has deformed those of her children who dwell along the barren shores, fighting a lost battle to exist on the hinterland's bleak fringes. What mutations—as if a nuclear war already had occurred. Insects have no wings; penguin birds cannot fly; the mammals—seals, whales and dreadful porpoises—are legless. And all battle interminably with one another and with death.

The blue whale hunts the shrimplike krill. Killer whales, extending long lizardlike heads, burst through the thinner ice in quest of penguins. The sea leopard, a predatory monster with serpentine neck, peers like some furry seaborne dinosaur searching for its prey.

Once, as enormous coal beds prove, this land mass was green with fern jungles and untenanted pine forests. Even today rudimentary lichens cling to the peaks protruding impassively above the snow. But life, as evolved on other continents, by-passed Antarctica.

Here is the victory of the Ice Age, whose inexorable intrusions have elsewhere been defeated by the sun. The sun in Antarctica is only ornamental. It lights up the strange mauve, pink and green shades these glaciers can reflect. But, in its deep and inner personality, Antarctica is a continent without color. Like the six-month night and six-month day that alternate above this emptiness, colorless black and colorless white are the true Antarctic shades. And these, depending on custom and tradition, are the hues selected elsewhere to dress death.

"Great God," wrote Robert Falcon Scott, who lost his life in 1912 after visiting the southern Pole, "this is an awful place." The wind roars without beginning and without cease, sometimes at two hundred miles an hour. The temperature can drop to −130°. Metal is rustless and wood does not rot. For death is the most sterile of conditions. Even the brilliant ingenuity and fierce determination of modern mankind have made but a tiny mark on death's morbid Antarctic kingdom.

Beast and man are damned when they intrude on death's Antarctic sovereignty, among its ferocious nunataks and névé, its sastrugi, its bergschrunds, its barrancas, its dongas, its hummocks and its séracs: that special vocabulary we have chosen for objects dimly discerned in death's private and forbidden whiteout, where land, sea and sky become invisible when death would keep its secrets to itself.

The condemned frustrated penguins fly beneath the water, using their wings as flippers to fight for life. These poor animals were once, by blundering and myopic old St. Mael, mistaken for a tribe of savages. When St. Mael baptized the gentle birds, risking frostbite to his withered fingers, Heaven was placed in serious predicament. How were these penguin souls to be received at God's right hand? The archangels met in council and decided there was but one way out of this strange quandary: that was to change the penguins into men. It has been done. Penguins no longer sin in innocence, for they have been well and truly damned.

Antarctica, of damned birds, is no fit human habitation. It is colder than those "Northern parts, all over Scandia," where, Burton tells us, men "are imprisoned half the year in stoves, they dare not peep out for cold." It induces delusion and bewilderment, that strange stare psychiatrists know as the Big Eye.

Death, terror and destruction dominate our empty, lonely South, a continent twice the size of teeming Europe. And, despite those scientific devices permitting man to stand upon a springboard and pock these eternal snows, death remains king. Here we remember the slogan of Antarctica, the words of Scott's lieutenant, Tryggve Gran: "How hard death must be for those who meet it having done nothing."

Bold, great men have trespassed death's domain. There is Captain Oates of the Inniskilling Dragoons, a "dry-humored, taciturn and imperturbable soldier," who tottered out deliberately to die in the frozen desert so his companions, escaping from the Pole, might have more food. "We knew that poor Oates was walking to his death," said Scott in his tragic diary, "but though we tried to dissuade him, we knew it was the act of a brave man and an English gentleman. We all hope to meet the end with a similar spirit, and assuredly the end is not far."

Scott himself, with two companions, struggled onward to the tent that proved to be their final resting place among the drifts. There, resigning himself at last to his bleak fate, Scott wrote achingly: "We are showing that Englishmen can still die with a bold spirit, fighting it out to the end. . . . Had we lived, I should have had a tale to tell of the hardihood, endurance and courage of my companions which would have stirred the heart of every Englishman. These rough notes and our dead bodies must tell the tale. . . . It seems a pity, but I do not think I can write more." Those who found them remarked of Scott: "It was evident that he had died last, and had died as he had lived, hard."

Ten years later, before his heart failed on the edge of the Antarctic, another explorer, Sir Ernest Shackleton, noted in his journal: "In the darkening twilight I saw a lone star hovering gem-like above the bay." Then, as he tossed sleepless, racked with pain, came death's clear call.

Death's suzerainty, alas, is not limited to Antarctica; nor are those trespassers who squeak across that eerie mass alone in seeking its thin hand. Within us we each bear our grim Antarctic and daily we traverse it, some courageously and some in trepidation, looking for guidance, for comfort and for the excellent

example of those numberless heroes who saw and
spurned death as they made their journey toward it:
spies and adventurers, kings and warriors, saints, sin-
ners, brigands, conquerors, freebooters, children, glow-
ing women and simple men. Each crossed his wasteland fearlessly, hour by hour.

Skarphedinn, besieged in a flaming fortress by his
Icelandic enemies, burned a cross into his flesh with
his battle-axe as he was dying, to show his contempt
for death's procedure. Hannibal, when surrounded,
called for poison, long kept in readiness, and said:
"Let us release the Romans from their anxiety, since
they think it too long to wait for the death of an old
man."

Kraljević Marko, slippered Serb, shared red wine,
eighteen liters at a time, with his piebald horse,
Šarac, before riding merrily off to die. Pavle Dokić,
last of the Jugoslav robber hajduks, spat at the gendarmes hunting him in 1938 and, as he lay wounded
in a bosk, completed a diary announcing:

"In Heaven there is one God and one Pavle Dokić
on earth. Only these two remain powerful. The world
will remember the last *hajduk*. I will have a step like a
youth. And I will travel like a hero. And will feed
like a wolf. I will be like God in Heaven; for now we
remain, only us two, He in Heaven and I on earth.
As we *hajduks* say, so must it be; and there will always
be us *hajduks*. For the forest without *hajduks* cannot
be, as Heaven without God. Here I have arrived this

lovely summer to freedom in the open spaces, to hear what I have most loved on earth, that players play for me a parade march and the Turkish *rastanak* and the *Gjurdjevski kolo* and *Tamo Daleko*. Sadness for others I have lived through. I have lived that the whole people know me. On all sides is my portrait." Like a wolf, like a youth, he stepped to death.

When the New England teacher Nathan Hale was taken as a spy, he scoffed at death upon the scaffold, quoting from Addison's *Cato*: "What a pity it is that we can die but once to serve our country." Impressed by his fortitude, the British general Howe gave orders to keep secret his manner of going so "that the rebels should not know they had a man in their army who could die with so much firmness."

By Washington's order, the Continentals executed the British spy Major André at Tappan in 1780. Says the journal of Dr. Thacher, Revolutionary surgeon in attendance: "It was his earnest desire to be shot, as being the mode of death most conformable to the feelings of a military man, and he had indulged the hope that his request would be granted. At the moment, therefore, when suddenly he came in view of the gallows, he involuntarily started backward and made a pause. 'Why this emotion, sir?' said an officer by his side. Instantly recovering his composure, he said, 'I am reconciled to my death, but I detest the mode.'

"While waiting, and standing near the gallows, I observed some degree of trepidation—placing his foot on a stone and rolling it over, and choking in his throat as if attempting to swallow. So soon, however, as he perceived that things were in readiness, he stepped quickly into the wagon, and at this moment he appeared to shrink; but, instantly elevating his head with firmness, he said, 'It will be but a momentary pang;' and, taking from his pocket two white handkerchiefs, the provost marshal with one loosely pinioned his arms, and with the other the victim, after taking off his hat and stock, bandaged his own eyes with perfect firmness which melted the hearts and moistened the cheeks not only of his servant, but of the throng of spectators. The rope being appended to the gallows, he slipped the noose over his head, and adjusted it to his neck with the assistance of the awkward executioner. Col. Scammel now informed him that he had an opportunity to speak, if he desired it. He raised the handkerchief from his eyes, and said, 'I pray you to bear me witness that I met my fate like a brave man.' The wagon being now removed from under him, he was suspended, and instantly expired. . . ."

Nurse Edith Cavell was shot in 1915 by the Germans in occupied Belgium. The Rev. H. S. T. Gahan, the British chaplain who attended her, reported "to my astonishment and relief I found my friend perfectly calm and resigned . . . during that last interview of almost an hour. . . . She . . . wished all her friends to know that she willingly gave her life for her country, and said: 'I have no fear or shrinking. I have seen death so often that it is not strange or fearful to me. . . . But this I would say, standing as I do in view of God and eternity: I realize that patriotism is not enough. I must have no hatred or bitterness toward any one.' "

Viking Brodir was seized by Wolf the Quarrelsome. His belly was cut open and he was led round and round the trunk of a tree. As his entrails fell about him, he watched with stony insolence. The regicide Radoje Janković, once a Jugoslav diplomat, told me how, when the Serbs retreated through Albania during World War I, they captured free-booters, tied them to trees and, to save ammunition, cut their throats. The Shqiptar Ghegs, who boast descent from eagles, uttered no sound. They held their long, lean bodies and aquiline features impassive to the knife. "These men knew death," said Janković. "They met it on even terms."

Enver Pasha, the Turkish revolutionist, died on the Russian-Afghan border under the sword cut of a Bolshevik agent named Agabekov, as unconcerned with death as he had been with life. When Gitanillo's femoral artery was severed by a Spanish bull, the matador told his father: "Don't cry, little papa. You remember how bad the automobile thing was and they all said we wouldn't get over it? This is going to be the same way. But tell them to moisten my mouth. Just moisten my mouth a little."

Lord Nelson, at Trafalgar, finally met the death he

long had courted. Amid the rolling waves and rolling thunder of the guns, a musket ball from the *Redoubt-able*'s mizzentop struck his left shoulder and he fell, saying calmly: "They have done for me at last, Hardy." "I hope not," cried the latter. "Yes," said Nelson, "my backbone is shot through." And, in the onrushing darkness, he inquired: "How goes the day with us?"

"Very well," said his aide. "I hope," Nelson whispered, "none of our ships have struck." Hardy answered: "There was no fear of that."

"I am a dead man, Hardy," Nelson observed. "I am going fast; it will be all over with me soon. You know I am gone. I know it. I feel something rising in my breast which tells me so."

The surgeon, Mr. Beatty, asked if the pain was great. "Yes," said Nelson, "so great that one might wish himself dead (but) one would like to live a little longer too." He commanded his ship to anchor as, one by one, the French battle fleet struck. He ordered: "Don't throw me overboard." Then, "Kiss me, Hardy," he murmured. "Now I am satisfied. Thank God I have done my duty."

He turned to the chaplain. "Doctor," said he with difficult articulation, "I have not been a great sinner." He repeated, "Thank God, I have done my duty," and expired.

Magellan, the circumnavigator, was slain by naked Filipino savages far from his native Spain, dying amid the twang of crossbows, the rattle of arquebuses, the fruitless bang of bombards, the smash of sea tides and the crackle of burning native huts. First he was wounded in the right foot by a poison arrow. Then came showers of stones and lance hurls. Twice his helmet was struck from his head. He was speared in the face and in the right arm, then slashed with innumerable cuts of sickle-shaped *terzados* until, as the chronicler, Pigafetta, relates: "the Indians threw themselves upon him, with spears and scimitars and every weapon they had and ran him through—our mirror, our light, our comforter, our true guide—until they killed him." And there was nothing but the sough of waves, the shouts of tribesmen and the lugubrious sounds of Spaniards retreating to their ships.

Cooper's Delaware chief died "with a look of inextinguishable scorn." Andrić's Bosniak, impaled by gypsies working for the Janissaries, muttered through clenched teeth from his dreadful stake on a bridge above the Drina River: "Turks, Turks, Turks on the bridge. May you die like dogs . . . like dogs." And Sienkiewicz's Tartar, Azya, spitted on a still more terrible instrument, his eye drilled out by a Polish sergeant in the silvery moonlight, soundlessly expired, giving his executioners no pleasure in their cruelty.

Marco Botzaris, of Sulion in Greece, died bravely on a village wall erected to defend only against foxes and badgers but tenanted by Turkish Ottomans armed with silver-ornamented pistols and long Albanian muskets. James Bowie, the American frontiersman, fought from his bed in the Alamo with a knife, and his body was pitched about on the bayonets of Mexican soldiers. At Bicocca (some say Sempach) Winkelried, the Swiss mercenary captain, opened a breach in Austrian ranks by gathering an armful of spears within his breast—and falling dead.

And on the Plains of Abraham, General Montcalm and General Wolfe found the death they long had wooed. Wolfe led a charge against Quebec until, shot three times, he staggered and collapsed. His officers proposed a surgeon but he said: "There is no need. It's all over with me." When he was told, "They run, they run," he inquired: "Who runs?"

"The enemy, sir," said an officer. "Egad, they give way everywhere." Wolfe turned upon his side and murmured: "Now God be praised. I will die in peace."

Montcalm, his gallant enemy, was borne by the wave of fugitives back toward town. A shot pierced him, blood poured, and a woman shrieked: "O mon Dieu! Mon Dieu Le Marquis est tué." To which Montcalm replied with his last breath: "It's nothing, it's nothing. Don't be troubled for me my good friends."

Hamilton, shot by Aaron Burr on Weehawken Heights, calmly instructed his sobbing wife before he died: "Remember, my Eliza, you are a Christian." Daniel Webster likewise expired nobly, saying: "Wife, children, doctor, I trust on this occasion I have said nothing unworthy of Daniel Webster." Gandhi, when he was assassinated, merely murmured, "Oh, God." The Constable Bertrand du Guesclin, that most gallant of Frenchmen, stricken by illness at Châteauneuf-de-Randon, gathered his knights about him and said lovingly and quietly: "Good lords and friends, I see well and clearly there is no escape from the malady I have and it is mortal." His barons heard him sadly, and then stormed the castle.

Lawrence, aboard *Chesapeake,* was shot on the quarter deck as he closed with *Shannon* out of Boston Harbor, standing conspicuous in his full-dress uniform, a huge man. As he was dying he gave his noble order: "Don't give up the ship." And Olga Dedijer, in June of 1942, fighting as one of Tito's partisans, had her arm almost severed by a German bomb on the Montenegrin height of Milin Klada. For nine days she staggered on as blood poisoning swelled her frail body. When they came to amputate on a dreary field where magpies picked the desolate earth for seedlings, one of the tattered surgeons offered her an ampule of heart stimulant. "Save it for those who will live," she murmured, dying. Her husband, Vladimir, dug her grave with a knife, clasped a great leaf upon his wounded skull, took Olga's revolver as a souvenir and marched to join his ever-retreating troops. And Rafis, "willing to die manfully, and escape reproach unworthy of his House, hee fell upon his sword; for haste, hee mist his stroke, and threw himselfe from the Castle wall; yet rose up againe, and ranne to a high Rocke, tooke out his owne bowells, and threw them among the people, calling upon the Lord of life and spirit, and so died."

Consider these intrepid personages who stared audaciously into death's eye socket: these heroes and these heroines, clad in iron, in furs, in silks, in breechcloths, in handsome uniforms and in rags. This splendid company: how boldly they trudge across death's continent, the famous and the valorous, the most noble, vanishing together into the night. Where are these audacious envoys, these beauties, these hapless chieftains, once so glorious, with bright teeth and eyes of clarity of heaven? Across what expanse and over what ledge have they disappeared from us?

They have gone to the threshold of thought, these toy animals with great spirits, to the threshold of being. "To be born is to leave the Nameless," says Lao-tse, "to die is to re-enter into the Nameless. . . . Who dies and, dying, does not protest his death, he has known a true old age."

These are the heroes who knew no age. "Man first puts on the grosser things of nature; his body is from them; but by death he puts these off, and retains the purer things of nature which are nearest to spiritual things: and these then are his continents." The continents of life and death.

To face death, since all men are alike condemned to die, is the beginning of mastery over life's terrors; to view death and to spurn it or accept it, either with equanimity, that is the justification. How easy is death for those who know how to meet it, striding across its silent iciness with pure, clean courage. We all have our Antarctic to traverse. Take heart from these splendid men and women, our colleagues and companions, who knew how to make the journey.

ELEVEN

The Beginning of the Moonpath

IN ONE OR ANOTHER way we are all familiar with death. We have seen the withering of a flower, the flopping of a beached fish, the frenzy of a butchered chicken, a de-spined sea urchin, sere leaf or lightning-shattered oak. We have regarded the corpses of friends, relatives and stricken strangers, the remains of men transformed into enemies by a uniform. We are saddened by death's aspect. Once I saw old Winston Churchill weep great tears, that doughty buccaneer, as he pointed to the body of a fledgling bird upon his doorstep.

Yet, though we are aware he inevitably waits for us, death almost always comes as a surprise. Everyone knows the tale of the Baghdad merchant who sent his servant out to buy provisions. The servant came back pallid and in great fear saying: "Master, just now in the bazaar I was jostled by a man in the crowd. I turned about and looked and I saw it was Death. He stared at me and made a threatening gesture. Therefore lend me your horse and I will ride away and thus avoid my fate. I will ride to Samarra where Death cannot find me."

The merchant lent his horse to the servant, who mounted it and rode off to Samarra as fast as he could gallop. And then the merchant himself went down to the bazaar and, as he strolled about, he too noticed Death standing in the throng. He approached Death and said: "Why did you make so threatening a gesture to my servant when you saw him earlier this day?" Death replied: "That was not a threatening gesture. It was merely a start of surprise. You see, I was astonished to find your servant in Baghdad because tonight I have an appointment with him in Samarra."

We are born with a reservoir of innocence and courage; and they fade proportionately. Knowledge uses up bravado; and bravery itself is but a limited capital which time erodes away. At twenty a man is not yet really afraid of death because he does not really believe in its existence, at least in terms of personal applicability. When he first learns the value of true danger and sees death's face, his fear and respect increase. He begins to contemplate the subject with morbid and unfriendly fascination and, if he is wise, he prepares to make death's intimate acquaintance.

This century, with its advantages of speedy travel

and inflated misunderstanding, affords death admirable facilities and all too many of us have brushed uncomfortably past him. Most men are given more than one opportunity to face death, or to imagine that they do so, which can be quite as testing. And often they astonish themselves by how they face it; some better than they might have imagined, and some worse. For the manner of death is often more surprising than death itself, and more important. To a degree we can control the style of our own dying even if we cannot influence death itself. One of life's few lessons ought to be fine dying.

Yet death upsets us when it slinks from Baghdad to Samarra. Some who would be ready to die bravely on land are fearful at sea or in the air. There is fear in the unfamiliar elements through which death strides. Then death is not death but acrophobia, death on a height; or agoraphobia, death in an open vastness; or claustrophobia, death in a cell or submarine. And this is unbalancing and unfortunate. For man, who cannot control his behavior at birth, would like the privilege of dying deliberately and well. It is the last flash of dignity we like to associate with what we call, in our simplicity, a link with the divine.

There are many ways of living, many trades: the Malayan fish listener, the Communist commissar to a track team, the specialist in soft-drink stocks, the grower of pyrethrum. Yet all of us, each practitioner of every trade, who enters life crying while others laugh, would like to depart laughing as others cry:

the last assertion of the lovely green nerve sap stored in our faded youth and extinguished with the luster of our hair, the calm courage called by some philosophy. "His life was glorious, his death bewailed."

We may prepare for death in the chamber of a hospital, reading the Dialogues of Plato and listening to Albenoni. But then mischievous death passes us by, waiting to catch us unawares. It prefers that iron rust first enter our souls; it prefers to seize us shivering, naked, howling in forlornness. Death chooses, by custom, to drain our vigor, to wear out our parts, to make our thoughts ragged and repetitive, to take us when we are old, useless and craven. What were the thoughts of venerable Noah when the time for dying started?

Death will reach out and snatch those impertinent men who have escaped to other planets. He has destroyed the great gods Khnum and Arecocha as he has destroyed those who worshiped their images. Generation after generation he destroys the devil-admiring Yezidi and the rigidly adoring monks of Athos, tending their shoats and capons. He has taken the great kings and the great commoners; Wittelsbachs, Hohenstaufens, Plantagenets, Hussainis; Tollemache-Tollemaches, Mavrocordatos, the Fuggers and the Welsers. His fierce sun has burned up desiccated pilgrims, tricked by the skippers of black-market dhows and left on the endless sands that do not lead to Mecca. From all believers death irreverently steals the lingering idols, trolls and selkies. And it will disintegrate each one of us like some wicked Chinese general scattering the bones of his dismembered enemies in Urumchi.

Our souls, like porters, often approach the dreadful gate unaware of its proximity. They crave the solace of eternal comfort and the assurance they cannot have. But this is the impossible promise. There have been no giants or immortals; nor will there ever be. Our dream is postulated but to quiet the anguish of our sorrowful flesh.

Take heed from Confucius: "In the morning, hear the Way; in the evening, die content." Take heed from Socrates: "No one knows but that death is the greatest of all good to men; yet men fear it as if they well knew that it is the greatest of evils. Is not this the more reprehensible ignorance, to think that one knows what one does not know?" Take heed from Epicurus: "Accustom yourself to thinking of death as nothing at all, since pleasure and pain exist only in sensation. It follows from this that a clear understanding of this fact that death is nothing allows us to enjoy this mortal life and at the same time obviates our speculating on the life eternal, relieving us of the regret of immortality. Because there is nothing to be feared in the fact that we live just as there is nothing to fear in the fact that we do not live."

The philosopher seeks posterity, not eternity. This is what sustained Madame Roland as she mounted the Revolutionary scaffold with unflinching eyes: the thought of living on in future memories. Dante counseled us: "All men on whom the Higher Nature has stamped the love of truth should especially concern themselves in laboring for posterity, in order that future generations may be enriched by their efforts, as they themselves were made rich by the efforts of generations past." It is comforting to give example in one's dying as well as in one's living; contemplate the sadness of those poor unfortunates who are obscurely hanged.

Perhaps men can never die happily until they have learned that the object of life itself is never happiness. Life and death run parallel courses and, as abstracts, can coexist for time immeasurable to our concepts even if they cannot coexist in individual bodies. It requires neither mysticism nor faith in the divine to believe that mankind as a species will survive this little Earth; for it requires even more human ingenuity to ferret out and destroy life in each terrestrial crevasse, on every mountaintop, than to find and establish permanent lodgment on another astral body. Nonetheless, as the strain of life persists elsewhere, the dark strain of death also persists, the darkness that inevitably can be escaped by no single creature. "More light," murmured Goethe as he died.

And so we approach the pantheistic end facing, beneath a Greek sky, the Olympian gods, all joyfully evil and related to us. About us spiders dance along their webs not knowing what flies they will catch before the dewy dawn. The ants crawl nonchalantly down their jagged holes; the sea breeze clutches for the midnight marrow. The inevitable moment comes

when we, who have always known that we must die but don't believe it, die.

Death's irreparable embrace reaches for these cells, joined in a cancerous growth called life. The answer approaches. We have always demanded explanation in terms we could try at least to comprehend, terms we have called God, a concept and a word we have invented. And now the answer comes, upon our little island.

Let us lie upon our backs and contemplate eternity, the Devil's own idea: mournful, dolorous and dreadful, a solitude multiplied by infinity. The church tower shakes and reverberates with pealing. There is a singing among the saplings and a strange perfume wafts upward in the dusk. "We renounce, O Lord, all our confidence in this world; for this world passeth away, and the lusts thereof." Farewell, fellow mariners, dear colleagues of the passage, pilgrims of the night. Naked as a goat my soul strides forth.

This is the beginning of the moonpath. There is a smell of tansy in the encroaching dark. The birds are preparing to flee southward from death's boreal threat. There is a stir among the insects. The world spins; the moments continue to whirl by. And there will be no trace of you, my friend, nor all the flummery of priests can keep you.

Already the pains are grasping at my liver. Already the pains are stabbing at my lungs and heart. My teeth fall out. My backbone shrinks. The follicles wither and the wrinkles spread. The energy seeps away in useless consternation. We entered in another's pain and now our own encompasses as we prepare to perish. Within my bad ear I can hear death's throb. The pipes are clogged; the bronchi filled with phlegm.

The death-fixated Peloponnesian Greeks assure you that a man's blood is supposed to shout out loud the day before he dies; and there is a shouting. I have not courted death nor do I welcome it; but nevertheless I feel its gravitational drag.

Ah, how delightful it would be to see again, within death's bleak and subterranean lands of Tartarus and Irkalla, behind its golden bar, below its pit, my dear friend Erszebet, who started as a goosegirl in Kiskunfélegyhaza; to embrace Firouzé in the velvet nights of Teheran and to regard, beside Galya, through a double-frosted window in dull Kuibyshev, Bactrian camels sliding across the frozen Volga; to drink again Byzantine wine of Melnik, Bavarian beer, the golden Pouilly of the Loire, or ruby claret; to catch ten more trout and one muskellunge and to strip and eat another fat grouse; to devour a Lim Fjord oyster, a cherrystone clam, sturgeon eggs in miasmal Astrakhan or Moussaka, as cooked by Marina and once consumed by greedy emperors above the Golden Horn; to hear the tinkling of Vivaldi and to drive a golfball long and straight; to eat kephtedes with my wife and children above Saint Friday's Bay; and once more to experience, if only for an instant, youth, grace, strength, delicacy and freshness. But this is not to be.

Old, withered and decrepit, they are going, we are

gone; and death will play no ferocious jokes with us. Each of us is now alone, we who have for moments thought we had escaped from solitude, through affection and creation, basking in evanescent, temporary glows of light along the dark path's edge. Now we see that throughout life truly we were alone, unable to communicate. But it was our life; and lord, how we hung on to it.

The years flaked off like dandruff; too late we call to them, hopelessly, like lost lovers: we who are become too old for desire and too experienced for curiosity, as Brother Death takes us in his arms.

The world banks steadily into the night. In the east the moon arises as a silver plate. There are a pattering and a rustling, a churning and a crashing, like the noise of waves that awaken the tired traveler who knows not where he is.

The wind and the rain come suddenly, with a jangling as of metal on metal, and there is a distant tramp, a beating in the tympanic membrane. The wind sweeps over the fields; and the stars; and the furrowed clouds. We clasp our arms about ourselves, holding tight, as the wind comes out of the north.

The way home is long. The grass bends with pity, the cypress tree bends with grief. And there is a strange sound, the sound of autumn that comes before a bleak and devastating winter. That stark naked fellow my soul stretches forth asking protection and boon. And now you know not, you know not, for there is not so dark a thing as light.

Everywhere the eternal drips and falls so slightly, while sounds steal. The ram shakes his skin. The moon fights free of the mouth of the pit. And, without taste, without smell, without eye, without ear, without speech, without understanding, without vigor and without breath, without mouth and without measure, inner or outer, one turns back again into time.

Here in Greece, where so much was begun, the Greece of Abraciot seers and Paphlagonian horsemen, where the cavalry rode forth in brave white corselets and the spearmen beat upon their shields, shouting Eleleu, Eleleu, to frighten the enemy's horses; where the perfumed ladies of Milos and Phocian whores enticed hoplites; and the Rhodian slingers flung stones at hollering barbarians flogging their men into battle; and the Hellenes oiled themselves with hog's lard, olive oil, sesame oil, oil of almonds and turpentine; and the Thracians pulled foxskin caps tight against their frozen ears; and charioteers in leather greaves and short white tunics, their hair bound long in clubs behind their backs, shouted to their stallions; and Cretan levies carried black-and-white shields of zebra skin against the bronze-tunicked Achaian warriors; here, where we savored the alcoholic honey of Trebizond, manufactured by bees who had drunk from the Pontic azalea and wafted from the Euxine Sea in galleys; where we tasted that of Hymettus, distilled from sweet and spiritual hives; where we sipped the red, resinated wine of Liopesi and the light *kokkinelli* of Attica beneath tall pines and among thick-growing pyracantha and lemon-fragrant verbena; ah, my warriors, where are they taking us who were once like flowers and young poplars?

Regard the Milky Way, that measureless galaxy which you will never see, that vacuum unpierced by either familiar sound or light, that knows neither the cruelty of fatigue nor the bitterness of pain, not even a cozy familiarity with horrid death.

There, to the east, the terrific sun is again arising between a cypress and a cypress. The sea is now slate gray and marked with white veins vertically streaking the wavecombs, whipped by a Spartan wind. And the cranes are taking off before the doves, leading them downward into Africa where pygmies, straddling goats, await them with deadly blowguns.

I am weary, infinitely weary. And spring is but a word and not a feeling; a beautiful woman is become a phrase. Corrosion withers my soul and eats my bowels. I shrink from its touch. And the future in which I lived, the scene of my hopes, is gone; and there is only past.

Now, come, my Brother Death; now, old, old, old, with hair like thistledown, I sink with fatigue into the soft Aegean waters that bear me northward and backward into time.

Spetsais, McMurdo Sound,
Korolevu, Paris, New York (1959-1960)

My thanks to Dr. J. Robert Oppenheimer and to Dr. Alvan L. Barach for their observations on scientific and medical meanings of death; to Mary Anne Leonard for her aid in preparing this manuscript; and to Lee Foster for his helpful editing.

C. L. S.

Bibliographical Notes

Sources used are listed approximately in the order in which they are quoted.

Chapter One
The Splendor of Death on the Mountain

BURTON, ROBERT. *The Anatomy of Melancholy.* Edited by Floyd Dell and Paul Jordan-Smith. Tudor Publishing Company, New York, 1955.

Sumerian tablet as translated by Professor Samuel Noah Kramer. *The New York Times,* May 25, 1959.

ERMAN, ADOLF. *The Literature of the Ancient Egyptions.* Translated by Aylward M. Blackman. E. P. Dutton, New York, 1927.

Ritual of the Mystery of the Judgment of the Soul, from an ancient Egyptian papyrus. Translated and edited by M. W. Blackden.

THUCYDIDES. *History of the Peloponnesian War.* Translated by Richard Crawley. Everyman edition, J. M. Dent & Sons, London, 1920. (Quotation from Pericles.)

The Works of Plato. Selected and edited by Irwin Edman. The Modern Library, Random House, Inc., New York, 1928.

Frazer, Sir James George. *The Golden Bough.* The Macmillan Company, New York, 1922.

Stenographic Record and Documents from the Trial of Dragoljub-Draža, Mihajlović. Belgrade, 1946.

Chapter Two
The Implications of Death

Plato. *Five Dialogues:* "Phaedo." Everyman edition, J. M. Dent & Sons, Ltd., London, 1952.

Plato. *Gorgias.* Translated by F. G. Plaistowe. University Tutorial Press, Ltd., London.

Hammond, William Alexander. *Aristotle's Psychology.* The Macmillan Company, New York, 1902.

Burnet, John. *Early Greek Philosophy.* Adam and Charles Black. London, 1908.

Titus Lucretius Carus. *De Rerum Natura.* With an English translation by W. W. D. Rouse. The Loeb Classical Library, William Heinemann, London, 1926.

Cursetji Pavry, Jal Dastur. *The Zoroastrian Doctrine of a Future Life.* Vol. XI of the Columbia University Indo-Iranian series. New York, 1926.

Dawson, Miles Menander. *The Conduct of Life (The Ethics of Confucius).* Carlton House, New York, 1915.

Rockhill, W. Woodville. *The Life of the Buddha.* Derived from Tibetan works in the Bkah-Hgyur and Bstan-Hgyur. Trubner & Company, London, 1884.

Herrigel, Eugen. *Zen in the Art of Archery.* Translated by R. F. C. Hill. Pantheon Books, New York, 1953.

Descartes, René. *The Philosophical Works of Descartes.* Rendered into English by Elizabeth S. Haldane and G. R. T. Ross. Vol. II. Cambridge University Press, Cambridge, 1912.

Spinoza, Baruch Benedictus. *The Ethics.* Translated by R. H. M. Elwes. Dunne, Washington, 1901.

Berkeley, Bishop George. *Principles of Human Knowledge.* The Clarendon Press, Oxford, 1891.

MONTESQUIEU, CHARLES LOUIS DE SECONDAT. *Pensées et Fragments*. Tome I. Gounoulhou, Bordeaux, 1899.
———. *Cahiers*. Tome I. Grasset, Paris, 1941.
ROUSSEAU, JEAN-JACQUES. *Emile*. Translated by Barbara Foxley. J. M. Dent & Sons, Ltd., London, 1925.
———. *Reveries d'un Promeneur Solitaire*. Musset-Pathay, Paris, 1882.
VOLTAIRE, FRANCOIS MARIE AROUET DE. *Oeuvres Completes*. Tome XXV. Garnier Frères, Paris, 1879.
FREUD, SIGMUND. *Beyond the Pleasure Principle*. Liveright, New York, 1950.
JONES, ERNEST. *Sigmund Freud, His Life and Work*. Vol. 3. Basic Books, Inc., New York, 1953-57.
DEWEY, JOHN. *Experience and Nature*. Columbia University Press, New York, 1925.
WAHL, JEAN. *Les Philosophies de l'Existence*. Armand Colin, Paris, 1959.

Chapter Three
The Halo of Death

MILTON, JOHN, "Lycidas."
DOUGLAS, NORMAN. *South Wind*. (Story of Saint Eulalia.) Dodd, Mead & Company, New York, 1925.
SCOTT, WALTER. *Ballads and Lyrical Pieces*. Archibald Constable & Company, Edinburgh, 1806.
LEONTIOS THE NAZEANZENE. *The Life and Liturgy of St. John of Cappadocia*.
ST. AUGUSTINE. *Confessions*. Vol. VI.
For accounts of Roman Catholic saints see *The Lives of the Fathers, Martyrs and other Principal Saints* by the Rev. Alban Butler, edited by Rev. Bernard Kelly. Virtue & Co., Ltd., London, 1949.

Chapter Four
The Death of Kings

FRAZER, *op. cit.*
BULPIN, T. V. *Shaka's Country*. Howard Timmins, Ltd., Cape Town, 1956.

VIRGIL, *The Aeneid.*

SUETONIUS. *The Lives of the Twelve Caesars.* The Modern Library, Random House, Inc., New York, 1931.

DUNN-PATTISON, R. P. *The Black Prince.* Methuen & Company, Ltd., London, 1910.

From Beowulf to Thomas Hardy. Edited by Robert Shafer. Vol. I. Doubleday, Page & Company, New York, 1924.

LANE-POOLE, STANLEY. *Saladin and the Fall of the Kingdom of Jerusalem.* G. P. Putnam's Sons, New York, 1898.

PRAWDIN, MICHAEL. *The Mongol Empire. Its Rise and Legacy.* Translated from the Russian by Eden and Cedar Paul. George Allen & Unwin, Ltd., London, 1952.

MALORY, SIR THOMAS. *Le Morte d'Arthur.* E. P. Dutton & Company, Inc., New York, 1957.

PRESCOTT, WILLIAM HICKLING. *The Conquest of Mexico.* E. P. Dutton & Company, Inc., New York, 1957.

VON ECKARDT, HANS. *Ivan the Terrible.* Translated from the German by Catherine Alison Phillips. Alfred A. Knopf, New York, 1949.

ZWEIG, STEFAN. *Mary, Queen of Scotland and the Isles.* Translated by Eden and Cedar Paul. The Viking Press, New York, 1935.

ROSS WILLIAMSON, HUGH. *The Day They Killed the King.* Macmillan, New York, 1957.

CASTELOT, ANDRÉ. *Queen of France, A Biography of Marie Antoinette.* Translated by Denise Folliot. Harper & Brothers, New York, 1957.

Chapter Five
Death in the Name of God

SINCLAIR, KEITH. *A History of New Zealand.* Penguin Books Limited, London, 1959.

KANT, IMMANUEL. *The Kritik of Judgment.* Macmillan, New York, 1892.

PRAWDIN, *op. cit.*

FRAZER, *op. cit.*

FISCHER, LOUIS. *The Story of Indonesia.* Harper & Brothers, New York, 1959.

FROUDE, JAMES ANTHONY. *Luther, A Short Biography*. Charles Scribner's Sons, New York, 1889.

DURANT, WILL. *The Story of Civilization: The Reformation*. Simon & Schuster, New York, 1957.

McINTYRE, J. LEWIS. *Giordano Bruno*. Macmillan & Company, London, 1903.

QUICHERAT, JULES. *Proces de Condemnation et de Rehabilitation de Jeanne d'Arc*. Tome III. Chez Jules Renouard et Cie., Paris, 1845.

HITLER, ADOLF. *My New Order*. Edited with commentary by Raoul de Roussy de Sales. Reynal & Hitchcock, New York, 1941.

Dachau the Nazi Hell. From the notes of a former prisoner at the notorious Nazi concentration camp. Arranged by G. R. Kay and translated by Lawrence Wolfe. Francis Aldor, London, 1939.

KOGON, EUGEN. *The Theory and Practice of Hell*. Translated by Heinz Norden. Farrar, Straus & Young, Inc., New York, 1951.

The Times. (Story of Sikhs in the Punjab.) London, August 8, 1947.

MALAPARTE, CURZIO. *Kaputt*. Translated by Cesare Foligno. E. P. Dutton & Company, Inc., New York, 1946.

VOLTAIRE, *op. cit.*, Tome IV.

Chapter Six
Death by Battle

Chants de Guerre de la Serbie: "La Bataille de Kossovo." Librairie Payot et Compagnie, Paris, 1916.

New York World Telegram. Dispatch from Italy by Ernie Pyle. January 10, 1944.

PRAWDIN, *op. cit.*

OMAN, CHARLES. *History of the Art of War in the Middle Ages*.

JOINVILLE, JEAN DE. *Memoirs of St. Louis IX*.

DEL CASTILLO, BERNAL DIAZ. *The Discovery and Conquest of Mexico*. Farrar, Straus & Cudahy, New York, 1956.

FÜLÖP-MILLER, RENÉ. *Leaders, Dreamers and Rebels.* Translated from the German by Eden and Cedar Paul. (Story of Ziska.) Viking Press, New York, 1935.

LIVY, *The History of Rome*, Book XXII.

The History of Herodotus. Vol. IV of *The Historians of Greece.* Translated by George Rawlinson. The Tandy-Thomas Company, New York, 1909.

Works of Flavius Josephus. Vol. II. Translated by William Whiston. Printed by S. Hamilton. London, 1811.

TOLSTOY, LEO. *War and Peace.*

STENDHAL. *La Chartreuse de Parme.*

EDMONDS, WALTER D. *Drums Along the Mohawk.* Little, Brown & Company, Boston.

LEWIS, LLOYD. *Sherman: Fighting Prophet.* Harcourt, Brace & Company, New York, 1958.

RICHARDS, FRANK. *Old Soldiers Never Die.*

HERSEY, JOHN. *Hiroshima.* Alfred A. Knopf, New York, 1958.

Chapter Seven
Death on a Pale Horse

Keesing's Contemporary Archives. Vol. V, 1943-46. (Starvation in Bengal and Pari.)

The New York Times. August 27, 1921. Article by Walter Duranty. (Quotation from Irenitskin.)

Ibid. September 6, 1921. Article by Floyd Gibbons.

WINSLOW, CHARLES-EDWARD AMORY. *The Conquest of Epidemic Disease.* Princeton University Press, Princeton, 1944.

BOCCACCIO. *The Decameron.* Translated by Leopold Flameng. London.

DEFOE, DANIEL. *A Journal of the Plague Year.* The Modern Library, Random House, Inc., New York, 1948.

CAMUS, ALBERT. *The Plague.* Translated by Stuart Gilbert. Alfred A. Knopf, London, 1948.

France-Soir. Paris, March 3, 1960. (Quotations from victims of Agadir earthquake.)

The New York Times. January 27, 1929. Article by Franz F. Oberhauser. (Quotation about Krakatoa.)

PLINY. *Letters.* Vol. I. Loeb Classical Library, William Heinemann, London, 1915.

Chapter Eight
Death by Man's Own Hand

WARD, REGINALD SOMERSET. *Maximilian Robespierre, A Study in Deterioration.* Macmillan & Company, Ltd., London, 1934.

The New York Times. August 22, 1940. Article by Arnaldo Cortesi. (Trotsky's murder.)

MONELLI, PAOLO. *Mussolini, An Intimate Life.* (Translated by Brigid Maxwell.) Thames & Hudson, London, 1953.

BULLOCK, ALAN. *Hitler: A Study in Tyranny.* Odhams Press, Ltd., London, 1952.

KOESTLER, ARTHUR. *Reflections on Hanging.* Victor Gollancz, Ltd., London, 1956.

WERTENBAKER, LAEL TUCKER. *Death of a Man.* Bantam Books, New York, 1957.

YOUNG, DESMOND. *Rommel, The Desert Fox.* Harper & Brothers, New York, 1950.

BURTON. *op. cit.* (Gismund and Guiscardus.)

BASHAM, A. L. *The Wonder That Was India.* Sedgwick & Jackson, London, 1954.

LLOYD, A. B. *In Dwarf Land and Cannibal Country.* T. Fisher Unwin, London, 1899.

Chapter Nine
The Anatomy of Death

LA FONTAINE. *Fables.* (Le Mort et le Mourant.)

DONNE, JOHN. *Devotions.*

BACON, FRANCIS. *Essays.* "On Death."

ANDREYEV, A. A. *Seven That Were Hanged.*

The Book of Signs, drawn and explained by Rudolf Koch, translated from the German by Vyvyan Holland. The First Edition Club, London, 1930.

POE, EDGAR ALLAN. *Tales of Mystery and Imagination.* "The Masque of the Red Death." "The Black Cat," "The Fall of the House of Usher," "The Case of M. Valdemar." Howard Wilford Bell, New York, 1904.

DOSTOEVSKY, FYODOR. *The Brothers Karamazov.* Translated by Constance Garnett.

HEMINGWAY, ERNEST. *Death in the Afternoon*. Charles Scribner's Sons, New York, 1932.
The Diary of Samuel Pepys. Vol. 5. Edited with additions by Henry B. Wheatley. G. Bell and Sons, Ltd., London, 1920.
KOESTLER, *op. cit*.
KOGON, *op. cit*.
BURTON, *op. cit*.

Chapter Ten
The Death We Face Within Ourselves

BURTON. *op cit*.
EVANS, ADMIRAL SIR EDWARD P. G. R. *South With Scott*. Collins, London, 1944.
SEAVER, GEORGE. *Scott of the Antarctic*. John Murray, London, 1940.
SULLIVAN, WALTER. Quest for a Continent. McGraw-Hill Book Company, Inc., New York, 1957.
MILL, HUGH ROBERT. *The Life of Sir Ernest Shackleton*. William Heinemann, Ltd., London, 1923.
TITUS LIVIUS. *The History of Rome*. Vol. IV. Translated by William A. McDevitte. George Bell & Sons, London, 1906.
SULZBERGER, C. L. *The Big Thaw*. Harper & Brothers, New York, 1956.
PENNYPACKER, MORTON. *The Two Spies: Nathan Hale and Robert Townsend*. Houghton Mifflin Company, New York, 1930.
André's Journal. Vol. II. Edited by Henry Cabot Lodge. The Bibliophile Society, Boston, 1904.
The New York Times. October 23, 1915. (Quotation by the Rev. H. S. T. Gahan.)
The Story of Burnt Njal. J. M. Dent & Sons, Ltd., London, 1911. (Viking Brodir.)
HEMINGWAY, *op. cit*.
SOUTHEY, ROBERT. *The Life of Nelson*.
ZWEIG, STEFAN. *Magellan, Pioneer of the Pacific*. Translated by Eden and Cedar Paul. Cassell & Company, Ltd., London, 1938.
COOPER, JAMES FENIMORE. *The Last of the Mohicans*.

Charles Scribner's Sons, New York, 1919.

ANDRIĆ, IVO. *The Bridge on the Drina.* Translated from the Serbo-Croat by Lovett F. Edwards. George Allen & Unwin, Ltd., London, 1959.

SIENKIEWICZ, HENRYK. *Pan Michael.* Translated from the Polish by Jeremiah Curtin. Little, Brown & Company, Boston, 1893.

FINLAY, GEORGE. *A History of Greece.* Vol. VI. Oxford University Press, Oxford, 1877.

PARKMAN, FRANCIS. *France and England in North America.* Little, Brown & Company, Boston, 1922.

OEUVRES DE FROISSART. Vol. XXI. Par M. le Baron Kervyn de Lettenhove. Comptoir Universel d'Imprimerie et de Librairie. Brussels, 1875.

ROOSEVELT, THEODORE. *The Naval War of 1812.* Vol. I. Statesman Edition, New York, 1882.

DONNE, JOHN. *Biathanatos.* Columbia University Press, New York, 1930.

Le Doctrinal de Lao-Tseu. J. Haumont, Paris, 1944.

SWEDENBORG, EMANUEL. *Divine Providence.* Swedenborg Society, London, 1934.

Chapter Eleven
The Beginning of the Moonpath

CONFUCIUS. *The Analects.* Translated and annotated by Arthur Waley. George Allen & Unwin, Ltd., London, 1938.

ST. JOHN OF THE CROSS.

The Works of Plato. Selected and edited by Irwin Edman. The Modern Library, Random House, Inc., New York, 1928.

Epicure, sa vie, son oeuvre, sa philosophie. Presses Universitaires de France, Paris, 1940.

DANTE ALIGHIERI, *De Monarchia.* Bk. I. Edited with translation by Aurelia Henry. 1904.

DONNE, JOHN. *Complete Poetry and Selected Prose.* Edited by John Hayward. Random House, New York, 1929.

About the Author

Cyrus Sulzberger is a newspaperman who has spent more than a quarter of a century in constant travel on all of the seven continents. He lives in Paris but is rarely there. Formerly head of *The New York Times'* foreign service he has for some years written a column on diplomatic affairs for that paper.

Mr. Sulzberger was born in 1912 in New York City, and graduated from Harvard in 1934. He is married to the former Marina Lada, and has two children.

The idea for *My Brother Death* germinated in the author's mind for a long time, and was written piecemeal in Greece, France and many other places.

Set in Linotype Electra
Format by Jean Krulis
Manufactured by The Haddon Craftsmen, Inc.
Published by HARPER & BROTHERS, *New York*